Tempest in a Teapot
and the
Den of Zen

Further Zen Ramblings from the Internet

Scott Shaw

Buddha Rose Publications

Tempest in a Teapot and the Den of Zen:
Further Zen Ramblings from the Internet
Copyright © 2017 By Scott Shaw All Rights Reserved

Cover Photographs by Scott Shaw
Copyright © 2017 All Rights Reserved

Rear Cover Photograph of Scott Shaw by Hae Won Shin
Copyright © 2017 All Rights Reserved

No portion of this book may be reproduced in any manner without the expressed written permission of the author or the publishing company.

First Edition 2017

ISBN 10: 1-877792-95-0
ISBN 13: 9781877792953

Library of Congress: 2017946303

Printed in the United States of America

10 9 8 7 6 5 4 3 2 1

Tempest in a Teapot and the Den of Zen

Introduction

Here it is, *The Scott Shaw Zen Blog 8.0,* originally presented on the World Wide Web. All of the writings presented in this book were written between February and June 2017.

As was the case with the previously published volumes based upon *The Scott Shaw Zen Blog;* entitled: *Scribbles on the Restroom Wall, The Chronicles: Zen Ramblings from the Internet, Words in the Wind, Zen Mind Life Thoughts, The Zen of Life, Lies, and Aberrant Reality, Apostrophe Zen, The Abstract Arsenal of Zen, and Zen and Again: The Metaphysical Philosophy of Psychology* this volume is presented exactly as it was viewed on scottshaw.com with no rewriting, punctuation, or typo corrections. From this, we hope you will receive the original reading experience.

This volume of internet ramblings is presented with the date and time listed as to when each blog was originally posted. Also, the blogs in this volume are presented from last to first. With this, we hope to present a transcendence back through time as opposed to an evolving evolution. In addition, we left out the traditional *Table of Contents* in an attempt to leave this volume with a much more free-flowing reading experience.

Okay, there's the information and the definitions. Read on… We hope you enjoy it. And, be sure to stayed tuned for the ongoing *Scott Shaw Zen Blog* @ scottshaw.com.

* * *
21/Jun/2017 08:30 AM

Nobody wants to hear that they are doing something wrong.

*   *   *

20/Jun/2017 08:22 AM

Did you take or did you give?

Did you take to have something to give?

If you take you owe somebody something.

If you give somebody owes you something.

Calculating Consciousness and the Illusion of Personality
20/Jun/2017 07:34 AM

It has happened to me more than a few times that I meet someone after they have seen my movies and they say, *"You are totally different from what I expected."* As some of them have continued, this is because they expected a very serious, intense person like I portray in my characters. But, I'm not like that at all. I'm all about the happiness and the laughter.

I explain this, and I use myself as an example, because people commonly perceive people via a method of expected judgment. They see something, they read something, they hear something, and they believe they know a person. But, they do not. You can only know a person when you know them one-on-one. And then, you can only truly know them after personally interacting with them for an extended period of time because each of us have many hidden layers of personality that are only revealed through time.

People commonly fall into the wrongful ideology that they have the ability, and some even believe that they have the right, to judge other people. But, if your judgment is faulty and incorrect, what does that say about your ability to read and, in fact, understand a person? As long as you put your personal judgment at the beginning of the equation you can never truly understand anyone.

There is the perceived perception of a person. Then there is who they truly are. For some, in certain circumstances, they project an element of their personality to fit the environment they find themselves within. From this, others decide if they will or will not like that person. The problem with this type of calculation is, as only a certain aspect of that person's personality is being revealed in that particular situation, the relationship may be begun or ended before a full presentation is available.

In other cases, some people are deceivers. They pretend to be something they are not. They may even be manipulators. What they do is nothing more than an elaborate ruse. Thus, it is very important to step beyond the realms of initial, first glance, judgment if you ever hope to truly understand anyone.

In other words, don't judge a person, come to understand a person.

*   *   *
20/Jun/2017 07:11 AM

How should you calculate if what you are doing is a service or a hindrance?

If the thought of you is involved anywhere in the equation what you are doing is not a service.

* * *
20/Jun/2017 07:08 AM

Even when you're wide awake you eventually want to go to sleep.

*　　*　　*
19/Jun/2017 04:07 PM

If it happens one time it is an accident.

If it happens two times it is a coincidence.

If it happens three times it is a warning.

If it happens four times it is a choice.

Start calculating the behavior of those you encounter.

*   *   *
19/Jun/2017 12:13 PM

A saint in one faith is a sinner in another.

* * *
18/Jun/2017 02:35 PM

Do you ever try to be consciously silent? To not speak and not communicate for a prescribed, extending period of time.

Nobody Thinks About the Consequences Until You Get Caught
18/Jun/2017 08:43 AM

  I was thinking about a friend of mine who made his living by selling pot. He had been caught a few times, paid some fines, but then he got caught with a substantial amount of weed and was sent to prison for five and half years. I can't even imagine what that must have been like for him. But, he committed a crime and he was punished for it. He eventually got out and he died a couple of years ago but not before he witnessed how marijuana was becoming, "Decimalized," and becoming more-or-less legal in some states. It must have driven him nuts.

  The fact of the matter is, most people live within the confines of acceptable behavior. They don't break the law. They make a living the way most of us do. There are others, however, who skirt the realms of accepted, lawful behavior, and try to chart a new course for themselves. Some even believe that they are on a mission. But, whatever the motivation, if you step beyond the realms of the accepted and the lawful, there will be consequences.

  Nobody thinks about these consequences, however. At least, they don't think about them until they get caught.

  I was watching the new episode of *Cops* on TV last night and the officer had pulled over a guy because he ran his plates and his insurance was expired. The guy's girlfriend pulls up in a car behind the officer, ranting and raving, and video tapping the situation with her phone. When she was later asked why she did it, she said she hated cops because you kill our people. The couple was African-America. But, not only did the driver have a warrant for his arrest but the cops found a bunch of drugs in his car that the guy was obviously selling, two loaded guns with additional loaded magazines, and masks that the officers believed were used in armed robberies. They arrested them both. So, something as minor as not having car insurance, (which is a crime), lead to their demise. Yet, the woman was mad at the cops while she was the one breaking the law.

I completely understand the current climate in the African-American community. They have experienced some very wrong treatment. In fact, if you look back to the 1992 L.A. Riots, it was not simply sparked by the beating of Rodney King—which the video tape image will forever be etched into all of our minds. (And think how many of those situations took place that weren't caught on tape). But, just prior to that, a Korean woman who owned a liquor store in Southcentral L.A. had shot a young black woman in the back for whatever self-motivated anger based reason. Anger is a bad thing! It makes people do bad things! Anyway, the Korean woman was arrested, was tried and was convicted. Then, a white judge let her skate, only giving her probation. That was just wrong. Thus, the riots.

For anyone who understand the Korean mindset, you know that they have the potential to possess a very altered frame of reference in terms of life. Now, I am, of course, speaking stereotypically but I can clearly say this as I have been intimately interactive with Korean culture for virtually my entire life. They all want to succeed at any cost. They all want to be the boss. They all want respect. And, they will lie, cheat, hurt, damage, steal to get what they want; then deny everything and go to church on Sunday and pretend to be a Christian. One thing that occurs from this mindset is that they open businesses, like liquor stores, in the low-rent districts of major metropolitan cities as the rents are cheap and they can make easy money.

Now, this is no different than the drug dealer. And, just like the drug dealer they may claim to be offering a service. But, are they?

You know, it has always been one of the catch phrases in the war on drugs in America that marijuana is a gateway drug. But, what does that mean? All drugs are a gateway drug. And, altered consciousness has the potential of leading one down the road to doing very bad things. Think how many people have been killed or injured by drunk drivers. And, alcohol is legal.

If you are selling illusion that illusion is always attached to a price that must be paid. And, this is the problem with drug dealers or liquor store owners that cater to people who are lost in a life with little hope. The fact is, these people should pay a price for their crime as no matter how much they deny it they are hurting people while they are making money off of their suffering.

Certainly, virtually every culture throughout time has found a way to get high. And, this is the excuse that many a drug dealer will use. But, if you are financing your lifestyle by illegal means, what do you think will be the outcome of your life? You may not like the law, but the law is the law. If you break it, you must pay the price. And, moreover, if you justify your existence by financing your lifestyle by selling something that has the potential to hurt people, what does that make you?

So, what does this tell us about life? I believe that it is really important for each of us to look beyond simply what we want for us. ...We all want what we want. That's just life... But, what we do to other people in the process of us getting what we want defines who and what we truly are. And, where we place our self in life defines what kind of life we will encounter.

Sure, people want to get high. But, why? Sure, some people provide them a way to get high. But, is that a service or a crime? Where you find yourself in time and in culture will be the definition of that. The one thing that is for sure, however, is that the doorway to the pathway to getting high is surround by criminal activity. Thus, there will always be people who will be paying a price both before and after the fact. It is better to live a life where you hurt no one and there is not a price to pay.

Why Would I Give You Money?
17/Jun/2017 09:11 AM

Recently, I've been thinking a lot about the interplay of human consciousness and they way people interact—how they behave towards one another and for what reason. As can be seen in this blog and the ridiculously voluminous amount of my other writings, I think people should think about the other person first and care about the other person first. Okay... Simple enough. But, now what? Here we are in life and we want to do what we want to do.

I guess it's because I've made a number of films that I am often contacted by people who want me to finance their film. First of all, I don't do that. Even if I was rich enough, which I am not, I have so often seen the downside of what happens next when somebody gives someone money to make a movie.

Personally, I salute creativity. I love it on all levels. Art is one of the greatest things of life. But, here comes the next step, how do you get that art created as, especially in the film game, as it does cost some money?

The great thing about the era we currently live in is that filmmaking has become very affordable. I often discuss the times gone past and detail how expensive it was to make movies fifteen or twenty years ago. Now, it is very cheap. Yet, people don't want to earn the money to pay for their own creation. They want someone to give it to them. Why is that? Why don't they want to own the inception, the implementation, and the ultimate result? Well, maybe they do what to own the result. They just want to live the experience on someone else's dime.

Again, this goes to the entire interplay of human consciousness and how a particular individual sees the world. I have known many filmmakers, in this current day and age, that get out there, get the money, and make their movies. And, they do it on their own. They don't go to *indiegogo* or any other place. They do it themselves. There is something very respectable in that. There is something truly artistic in that. They have an artistic vision that they want to create and they get it done without turning to people they do not know to accomplish it. From this, whatever they create is free from the karma of, *"Owing."*

As I feel that I am often forced to state, "I pay for all of my films with my own money." Do I wish someone would give me a million dollar to make a movie? Sure! Hell, even a hundred thousand could make a great movie. With my experience in the game I could probably go out there, sell myself, and ask people to give me the money to make a movie, but I don't.

I think if you want art to be true art, especially in the early stages of your artistic career, you really need to prove that you care enough about your art to make it happen by yourself. That is the mark of a true artist.

So, how does this impact the study of human consciousness? If you seek outside people to make you what you are, how can you ever be yourself? Being yourself is the ultimate statement of an artist. Caring enough about the art that you hope to create to find a way to create it on your own, that is ultimate statement of artistic freedom.

*   *   *
16/Jun/2017 01:58 PM

Killing time… What happens to the time you've killed?

Stand Up for the Rights of the Creator
16/Jun/2017 01:57 PM

I was teaching one of my classes on filmmaking earlier today. As the class only meets once a week I try to keep the student very active in actual film creation so I generally give them an assignment to make a short film for each class session. This week's assignment was to do a visual biographical piece. One of my students did, what so many people have done before, was to intermingle footage of his life with footage from very famous films. The short had him talking to various characters from various films. This is always a fun presentation as you get to peer into the mind of the person and view how they see themselves in association with life. It was a good piece.

After his presentation he asked if I thought he should upload it to his YouTube page. I said he could but he may run into copyright problems.

Now, for anyone who knows me understands, I am an avid proponent of Intellectual Property Rights. If somebody made something they are the only one who owns it and other people can only use it if they are given permission.

But, more than that... Each person should have the moral dignity to ask the creator of a, *"Something,"* if they can use all or part of it. Maybe the creator will say, *"Yes."* Maybe the creator will say, *"No."* But, every person who wants to tap into the creation of another person's creativity should have the <u>honor</u> to ask if they can use it. That is just the right moral code of life. And, that is what I explained to my students.

Now, not everyone who infringes on another person's copyright gets sued. It's expensive and it's time consuming. Not every copyright infraction is reported to the FBI. So, some people get away with it. But, should they?

Have you ever asked the creator of a project, that you have stolen all are part of or have downloaded it for free from an illegal offshore website, how they feel about what you have done? If you haven't, what does that say about you? And, as I always state, if you were the one creating the something that is being stolen I am certain you would have a very different opinion about what is taking place than you being the thief.

Many people do not personally create books, movies, music, or art. But, they like it. So, they want to view it. But, have you ever had somebody steal your bike, your car, your wallet, or break into your house. If you have experienced that feeling, then you will know what the artist goes through when their creation has been stolen.

Okay… Okay… I won't go off here… ☺ But, as you can plainly see, I am really against people stealing other people's creations.

What I always suggest (like I did to my class) is be more than the thieves. Stand up for the rights of the creator. Understand that it took their creative vision, their time, their money, their mental focus, and their undaunted dedication to make that piece of art. Don't steal it!

The Funky Cuts Barber Shop
16/Jun/2017 08:16 AM

Recently, in this blog, I discussed a movie that I was in that was filmed in the Philippines but never saw the light of day. That was not the only one. I did a big movie in Japan that I have no idea of what ever became of it. Here in the States, I also did a couple of films, with fairly high budgets, and I have no idea what happened to them, as well. As an actor, I have had small roles that I performed end up on the cutting room floor. This is not unusual as big productions film a lot of footage and add a lot of small characters. Some of those characters make the cut, some do not. I would, of course, have liked it to go the other direction but it was not my rodeo so I had no say in the matter.

That fact is, there are a lot of films that are made, I have known of some productions with major stars attached, but they never found their way into distribution. It's just the nature of the beast. These facts are something that many people outside of the industry do not understand.

This is one of the main reason I got into production so early in my career, I wanted a say it what happened to the movie. This is also a lesson I teach my students as a filmmaking instructor and a warning I give to newbie actors who arrive in Hollywood—many a low budget production may go up but very few are finished. In fact, this is one of the primary reasons that I developed Zen Filmmaking. Yes, it initially organically arose out of the collaboration between Donald G. Jackson and myself when we were making Roller Blade Seven but from there I formalized it. Where Don was chaos, I was organized chaos. ...I did this so those filmmakers would have a method and means to actually get their film finished and not allow it to get lost in all of the over-reaching dreams and aspirations that many a young filmmaker has that cause them to shut down their production and not finish their movie.

All this being said, last night I remembered back to one of my first starring roles. It was a senior project made by a filmmaker graduating from USC. It was called, *The Funky Cuts Barber Shop.*

Here in L.A., prior to the domination of the internet, producers would put out casting notices in a weekly newspaper called, *Dramalogue.* Every week, all of the new and the established actors could bypass their agent and submit to these productions. I did it too. Thus, I got the lead role.

As schools like USC (obviously one of the major filmmaking school in the country) teach advanced levels of filmmaking, the students who attend need to make their own film productions. These student films were and are a great place for new actors to get their feet wet. Again, as I always tell my filmmaking students, these student films are in many ways a far better place to get your acting chops perfected because, unlike low budget films, they are assured of being completed as they have to be if the student wants to pass the class.

Anyway, the film was a fun introduction into the realms of no-budget filmmaking. In fact, I got to work with a very established actor, who had co-starred in a number of major films. Not to mention even members of the band Parliament/Funkadelic can be seen in the film playing music. It was a good experience.

A few months after filming I got a call from Brian, the director, telling me about the screening. It was the end of the year screening for all of the graduating USC students of that class. It was a big event with a lot of people in attendance. There were several films shown and then came, *The Funky Cuts Barber Shop.* I got top billing, even over the more established actor. It was a great feeling. Afterward, people I didn't even know were telling, *"Great job. Great performance."* Total ego booster. ☺

In any case, Don and I went up on *Roller Blade Seven* a short time later. I really took the sensibilities that I learned while working on this film into the production of Roller Blade Seven. Realizing that you do not need big money to make a fun movie you just need people that care.

But… Back to the point of all this… Just like the films I was in that were lost to *Hollywood never-never-land,* this film too is lost to the archives of the film vaults of USC. I saw it once and never saw it again. So, if any of you people out there know about how to tap into those vaults and get me a screening, I would love to see it again. I'm thinking it was for the class of 1990?

*   *   *
16/Jun/2017 08:15 AM

Believing that you know what another person is thinking is the sourcepoint for many of the world's biggest problems.

*   *   *
16/Jun/2017 07:45 AM

What contribution are you making to society?

* * *
16/Jun/2017 07:43 AM

When you say something negative about a person, what does that equal?

Does it make you a better person or does it simply make you look like the lessor person?

*   *   *
16/Jun/2017 07:43 AM

What does what you do actually equal?

* * *
16/Jun/2017 07:43 AM

You always sell your soul without knowing it.

Fix What You've Broken First
15/Jun/2017 04:53 PM

Maybe it's because I live in a large urban center like Los Angeles or perhaps it's because I'm involved in the film industry but I frequently encounter people who have had some pretty dastardly deeds done to them. From this, they are left with a scar on their life. They are left not as whole as they were before the negative action happened.

In all walks of life, people encounter those who do bad things. Why they do them is anyone's guess because nobody wants anything bad done to them. Thus, this should be their motivation to not do bad things to other people. Yet, they do.

Moreover, everywhere we turn these days, on the news it is constantly reported, all of the bad things that are taking place to people across the globe. Why would any one want to add to that?

On the other side of the issue, there are those who set up their life to encounter negative reprisals. They create a world of conflict all around them. They say bad things, they do bad things, they judge people, they hurt people, and they do not care. That is, they do not care until their karma bites them in the ass and the negativity they have unleashed is redirected their direction. Then, instead of understanding why bad things are happening to them and that they are, in fact, deserving of it, they become the victim. *"Oh, whoa is me..."*

Everyone wants the other person to be paid back for their bad actions but no one wants to be paid back for their bad deeds.

The fact is, most people don't intentionally do bad things. Sure, we all make mistakes and people get hurt in the process but these, *"Hurts,"* are generally minor. They are not wide spanning nor are they long-lasting. When we do them we apologize and try to fix what we have broken.

Unfortunately, not everyone is like this. There are those people who want to hurt people. They find some kind of misdirected superiority in their actions. As wrong as they are, this behavior goes on all the time, all over the place.

It has been highly documented how some people actually set about on a course to hurt people via the internet and how these actions have caused some of these victims to take their own life. Sadly, I knew a young girl who this happened to. I spoke about the incident in a blog a year or so ago. That's the thing, something like the internet is so wide spanning and it is so easy to generate so much hate and that hate has the potential to truly damage a person's life. I've seen this occur in my own life and in the life of several people I know. Thankfully, none so dramatic as my poor friend who took her own life, but doing bad things can begin with just a few key strokes.

Even in the world of the martial arts, as I have documented in a few articles, there are those low level practitioners, (if you can even call them martial artists), that go about creating hate by attempting to cast shade on other enthusiasts. That's just sad. The martial arts should be a tightly knit group that helps one another and is not infested by people who spread lies and hate.

What I am saying is that badness—doing bad things goes to all levels of life, even places that you would not expect it to occur. Though it should not, it has the potential to happen to anybody.

At the root of all you experience in life is what you have chosen to do. What you choose to do today sets your tomorrow into motion. With this understanding as a basis, I believe for each of us we really need to look to our lives and bring into focus the people that we have hurt. Whether it was intentional or not, that injury must be focused upon.

Initially, ask yourself, have you fixed the damage that you caused to that person? Perhaps your answer is, that you believe you were justified in the words you spoke and the actions you took that hurt the life of that other person? If this is the case, you are lost forever. Just like if you make excuses, find justifications, feel you had the right, or simply don't care about the people that you've hurt, then all that hurt breeds is damage coming your direction farther down the line. If you instigated it, you are responsible. There is no rationalization or justification that will remove you from this truth.

The main point of this piece, as the title implies is, *"Fix what you have broken."* It doesn't matter if you think you were right. It doesn't matter if you feel you were justified in the actions you took. If you have hurt someone, you have hurt them. Thus, that damage will not only forever haunt the person you hurt but it will forever haunt you until you make it right. Fix it!

The Who You Do The What To
15/Jun/2017 08:18 AM

Do you ever stop and ask yourself, *"Why am I doing what I am doing?"*

To begin, most people rarely, if ever, do this. They have an idea in their mind, an outcome they desire, and from this they just do. They do not think about the consequences of their actions, they simply want something that their doing will supposedly equal and thus they move forward.

If you do not consider the wide spanning consequences of your actions you are operating your life from a very selfish place as every word you speak, ever action you take creates consequences. Not only for yourself but for anyone and everyone else involved.

Many people do not take the time to think about what they are doing because they do not care. Most operate their life from a very unenlightened perspective and, as such, they are motivated solely by obtaining their desired end-goal; whatever that desire end-goal may be. As they do not think about the greater ramifications of their actions, not only to themselves but to others, they then find themselves forced to rationalize and justify what they have done.

On the level of survival, people all the time justify what they do to make a living, *"I have to support my family."* They do this while the job they do may be hurting themselves; i.e. in the case of coal miners and people who work with toxic substances onto the damage that the job they do may be doing to other people and to the earth. They simply dismiss any responsibility that they have in these matters as what they are doing is a commonly accepted vehicle of employment and, as such, they face no immediate personal repercussions. But, the repercussions do eventually arrive.

On the level of what people desire, this case becomes a lot more complicated. They are doing what they are doing for themselves, motivated by a specific set of desires. *"I want to be rich." "I want to be famous." "I want that girl or that guy."* And, the list goes on and on; from very large goals to very small things. People do what they do because they want something. Once they are lost in that desire they never take the time to think about what their desire is not only doing to their own life but what it is doing to the lives of others.

There is no point in life that what you do does not affect someone else. This is especially the case if you knowingly impact the life of someone else either by what you say or what you do. Ask yourself, *"Do I ever consider the other person before I do what I do?"* Your answer to that question describes how you interact with life.

The doing what you do to other involves three distinct personality types. First, there is the person who does what they do and does not care about the consequences to anyone else. Second, there is the person who does what they do and when they are confronted with the fact that what they have done has negatively affected the life of someone else they make excuses about their actions. Third, some people who are doing what they are doing and then they are forced to stop, for whatever reason, then look for reasons to recommence even though they now understand the actions they were taking are unwanted and are having a negative effect upon the life someone else. Which of these patterns do you fall under?

Here's the thing… Most people never even consider the effect they are having on others and the world around them. If this thought does cross their mind, they dismiss it or they find friends and family to provide them with the mental, (I won't use the word moral), support to continue on their path of fulfilling their desire no matter what the fulfillment of that desire may do to another person or the entire world.

Again, ask yourself, *"Why am I doing what I am doing?"* Now, add the question, *"How is what I am doing affecting the life of someone else?"* Look small, to the lives of individuals you may be affecting and then view the larger picture. If what you are doing hurts anybody—negatively affects the life of even one person, the essence and the source of that negativity grows and spreads out from that small source to encompass and engulf the greater whole of all that you pursue.

The fact is, you should think about other before you do anything. You should care enough to ask a specific person, who may be involved in your actions, how they feel about your actions. But, will you? Or, will you simply find excuses and justifications, maybe even seek the support of your friends and family, and do what you do without caring about the effect?

Look at life, who are the people that ultimate emerge as respected entities? They are the ones who did not base their life upon climbing on the shoulders of any person. They are the ones who did not hurt anyone in the process of their ascent to notoriety.

Like I always say, care enough to care. This should be your number one mantra. Care enough to think of others and to think of the greater repercussions of your actions before you ever set any desire into motion. If you want to achieve your goals, do it while hurting no one.

Abstract Understanding
and Why You Think You Know What You Know
14/Jun/2017 09:07 AM

Kind of picking up from the previous blog, a question you should ask yourself at each stage of your life is, *"Why do I think I know what I know?"*

Do you ever ask yourself that question? Do you ever ponder why you believe what you believe? Do you ever take the time to explore the inner workings of your mind and come to a conclusion of what is the basis for your beliefs?

You can think anything you want to think. You can believe anything you want to believe. You can come to any conclusion that you desire. But, that does not make it the truth that only makes it, at best, a personal belief.

People commonly mix up the concepts of belief and fact in their mind. They come to a conclusion, for whatever reason, and then they hold fast to that conclusion, believing it to be the truth. For some, they then speak that belief as if it were the truth. From this, some people also come to believe what another person believes. Not fact, only belief, but few people are ever able to spate the two.

It is essential to understand that believing is different from knowing. Believing is something that you hold within yourself—a personal realization if you will. ...A thought that you came upon and then decided to believe.

Knowing, however, is based upon a completely different set of standards. Knowing is defined by possessing a factual basis for what you believe. How do you come to that level of understanding? You do it by actually taking the time, doing the study, going to the source, and then discovering a factual truth based upon empirical reality.

Most people don't want to take the time to do this, however. Most people don't have the inclination to do this. At best, they read the books (for lack of a better metaphor) and then conclude what they believe to be the truth based upon the predetermined judgmental mindset that they brought to the table. Not fact. But, this is how most people operate and this is what gives birth to the system of their beliefs.

It is almost impossible to make anyone believe anything that they do not want to believe. It is almost impossible to make anyone change their mind once they have found something to believe in. Understanding this, you should operate your life within that perspective. To avoid conflict, you can let people believe what they wish to believe.

This does not make what they believe right. It does not make it the truth. It only makes it what they believe.

What do you believe? Why do you believe it? Is what you believe based in fact or is it based in mental fiction. Your life. Your choice. But, if you want to know the truth about any subject you need to go to the source, take the time to do the study, and find the true answer.

How Little You Know of the Truth
13/Jun/2017 09:15 PM

I was having coffee with a friend of mine this afternoon and another friend of ours happened by. We are all in the film game so we were discussing filmmaking. The guy who showed up late made the joke, *"Shouldn't we discuss something else?"* His joke made me think of that scene in the industry parody movie, *The Player,* where one of the main characters suggested the same thing. In the film, everyone at the table then goes silent as they looked at each other for a moment. Then, they all laughed and realized they knew nothing else to talk about. Certainly, my friends and I are not like that but the joke did send me to remembering…

We were talking for a while and then the one guy remembered he had seen some discussion on the internet about Zen Filmmaking and he wanted to know if what one person said was true. He asked if I wanted to see it. I said, *"Not really,"* but he pulled it up on his phone and showed it to me anyway. Once again, as I am so often reminded, people talk and talk on the internet but they have no factual basis for their discussion; i.e. what the aforementioned poster said was false. The fact is, if the people weren't just flat out insulting Zen Filmmaking, Don or myself, pretty much every observation and every supposed fact they were stating was simply wrong. What else is new? Welcome to the internet.

Personally, I don't really care but it is a good thing to use an example. Mostly, I think it is so sad that people use the unsubstantiated words of other people as a basis for their own so-called knowledge. …Knowledge that is not based in fact, it is simply based in interpersonal bullshit. That is <u>not</u> knowledge!

I always believe in people but time-after-time I am let down as I witness that most of what people speak is nothing more then self-propelled sources of emotional outbursts based upon what is missing in their own life, (as well worded as some of those outbursts may be), and/or simply flat out unsubstantiated opinions that are presented as fact. But, these people don't know the facts! They don't know me and they didn't know Don, so how can they have any true understanding about Zen Filmmaking or what motivated the various Zen Films?

I wrote a piece that touched on this a little while back, *"Zen Filmmaking: The Good, The Bad, and The People That Don't Know What the Fuck Their Talking About."* But, it seems that nothing ever changes, people want to gain fame by analyzing the works of other people; i.e. in this case me. They want to improve on their lacking sense of self-importance by looking like they know what they're talking about. But, they don't! All they speak is simply based upon emotion and judgment. And, that is the most horrible place to be operating from.

If what you say or what you do causes one person to say or do one negative thing then you are the source of an avalanche of negativity as that emotion will breed. Just as if you are the source for one person to say or do a positive deed you are the source for an avalanche of positivity. Looking at your life, looking at your karma, which do you think is better? But, most people don't think, they just act and react. Again, this is not a good place to be operating from.

I don't mean this blog to be about me. Because it really is not. And, I've stated my case about what I believe a million times. But, I mean this style of unsubstantiated bullshit is all over the internet; about every subject and every person. People should be more than that! People should be caring and doing actual verbal and physical things for other people that will very precisely make the life of other people better. But, I guess some do not have the mental aptitude for that.

Anyway… If I can take it back to a personal perspective for a moment to illustrate that point… None of these people who speak about me do anything for me. Are they making my life any better? No. Do they even thank me for providing them with a basis for something to discuss? No. So, what is their purpose? What is the purpose of their life? If all you do is discuss something else or someone else, that you have no true knowledge about, that leaves you with nothing more than a life based upon someone else's reality and your interpretation of it. Thus, all you are is a slave.

You know, I always tell everyone to go out and make your own art. Do what it is in life that you really want to do. Be your own person. Find your own greatness. But, you will never do that by climbing up on the shoulders of someone else. All that does is make you bound to that relationship.

Now, people who partake in this style of internet activity generally spread their ideals and opinions all across the internet. If any of you have ever been on the receiving end of an internet lie or an internet attack, then you probably will understand what I am speaking about when I say all it does is created a lot of wasted emotional energy. But, who created that melodrama? Was it you? Probably not. It was the other person with nothing better to do than to attack your life. And, that is just wrong!

So, what does this leave us with? If you are reading this blog you are probably a person who takes caring about other people and human consciousness seriously. You are probably not out there judging and placing your faulty interpretations and fraudulent facts onto the life of others while trying to make yourself famous by dong so. Thus, you are probably not damaging the life of others. And, that is good! You have not fallen prey to the illusion of the lawless internet.

The fact is, what you do in life; what you say, effects not only you but everyone. It creates your reality and it influences the reality of those you talk to and those you talk about. It creates your karma. If all you do is waste your time judging and talking about things you do not truly understand than you will find yourself at the end of your days having accomplished nothing and having helped no one. Is that where you want to end up? Or, if you choose to be sucked into the world of not caring about what you do or whom you may hurt then your life will follow your own self-proclaimed path towards destruction. That's just the way it is.

At any point in your life have you ever taken a moment and actually put your own emotions aside and stood up for someone you were mad at or didn't like? Try it. Believe me, it will change the way you view the world.

As I always say, care more about others than yourself. Take others into consideration before you do anything. Never hurt anyone. From this, not only will your life become better but the whole world will become a better place, as well.

Care before you do. Think before you speak.

The Biggest Sinner of Them All
13/Jun/2017 08:42 AM

Yesterday, I was doing what we do here in L.A., driving from one place to another. On the radio was Deepak Chopra. He was on Steve Jones', (of Sex Pistols fame), radio show, *Jonesy's Jukebox* on KLOS. Chopra apparently has just had a new book published and he was promoting it on the radio station. Good for him. He was discussing the typical mumbo-jumbo that many an Indian guru has proclaimed for centuries. To paraphrase: people have it all wrong we are not anything important, the universe is so big, earth is just a speck of sand, and we as human beings are lost in an illusion; we are not a whole person onto ourselves but we should work on becoming one with the greater cosmos. Nothing new in any of his words… I have heard these words spoken by so many people for so many years and have read so many books that have been written saying the same things.

…Maybe these words are new to the people who listen to KLOS as it a rock n' roll radio station locked somewhere in the mindset of the 1970s. But, these words have all been said before. Chopra is simply the current and most famous person speaking them today.

The problem with all of this is, it is the same metaphysical nonsense that has been handed down by all of the various religious scholars and metaphysicians forever… They are describing the something we are not—the something we should become—the something unobtainable, out there. They claim, we are all wrong as who and what we are and we need to become something more, better, and different.

Now certainly, becoming a better, more caring person is a good thing. Certainly, helping people is a good thing. But, the biggest mistake that all of the metaphysical teachers make is that they discus an abstract reality that is not part and parcel of physical existence. By doing this, they allow certain people to claim spiritual superiority. *"I have achieved this. You have not."* From this, certain people with a spiritual inclination spend their entire life attempting to achieve that abstract reality. Some call it enlightenment or nirvana. But, all these so-called teachers have done is set up the impossible equation. From this, a person who follows this path, or anyone for that matter, can never be good enough—they are never whole and perfect onto themselves.

    I remember back to a time when I was a teenager studying with the late Vietnamese Zen Buddhist monk, Thich Thien-An. He made a statement to me once when he was speaking of enlightenment, *"...Those who have found enlightenment..."* Meaning, he was not. I was so surprised to hear these words coming out of his mouth as he missed the whole point of nirvana. The greatest illusion is that there is no illusion at all. We <u>all</u> are already enlightened. We simply have to let go and know.

    And, this is the problem with teachers who propagate this metaphysical universe and the abstractness of the Out-There-ness. They keep people from being whole—being perfect on themselves. They keep people from understanding the perfection of the moment. They keep people from finding their own enlightenment. They do this by teaching all kinds of theories to keep people locked in the illusion that there is so much to know that they can never understand. ...That they will never be pure enough to understand. They make people believe that only the teacher who is teaching holds the answers.

    I call, bullshit. It is just another way for another person to make money off of the unsuspecting masses.

    Be free and you are free. Be good and you will understand why goodness is better. Be kind and you will understand why kindness is better. And mostly, don't lock yourself into believing that the something out there is unattainable.

Life is unknowable. That is the beauty of it. None of us will ever completely understand life. If you lock your mind into contemplating what you are not and what you need to become, you will never be the perfect you. Don't let these people suck you into that illusion. Don't let them make you focus on the, *"Out-there,"* that is unknowable. That's the beauty of it! It's out there, you can never know it! Just be the best you that you can be. Be good. Help people. Don't hurt anyone for any reason. And, realize that enlightenment is easy. All you have to do is let go of the illusion that there is something more you need to learn—something more you need to become. And, there you will find it.

Be good. Be free. Be enlightened.

* * *

11/Jun/2017 02:20 PM

Is your life defined by the time on the clock?

What if the time on the clock is wrong?

* * *

10/Jun/2017 02:58 PM

How much time do you spend thinking about the negative things you've done to other people?

How much of your time do you spend undoing the negative things that you've done to other people?

Even if you feel you were justified in your actions, that is only your opinion and your opinion is not a universal truth. Thus, you had no justification.

How much of your time do you spend thinking about the positive things you've done to other people?

How much of your time do you spend telling other people about what you did and who you helped?

If you are the one voicing what you have done, that means no one else is in agreement with your belief. Because if they were, they would be the one speaking. Thus, it is only your opinion that you have helped people and your opinion is not a universal truth. Which means, you have helped no one, only yourself via your ego.

Good people don't hurt people no matter what may be their justification.

Good people help people and because they do so from a space of purity, they seek no reward.

Even When You Think You Are Helping Others You Are Actually Helping Yourself
10/Jun/2017 07:32 AM

Whenever someone is supposedly doing something for someone else they are considered good and giving. This is especially the case for people who do things for people in need: be they homeless, ill, elderly, or injured.

Though giving is giving and caring is caring, there is a much bigger, more intricately designed mental actions taking place than simply the art of the doing. This is something that most people never take into consideration. They don't take it into consideration when they are complimenting a person who is doing something for someone nor do they take the time to look deeply within themselves when they are feeling good about themselves in relation to the fact that they consider themselves so kind and so caring when they are doing for those in need. That bigger issue is, when people are taking the time to do for others, they are actually doing for themselves.

There are several reasons for this and few people ever take the time to study their reason why or have the mental attitude to actually be able to look deeply within themselves and come to understand why they do anything that they do. People are self-motivated creatures. Yes, they do for others. Yes, they take the time to care but they do it so it will activate that place within themselves that brings them happiness, joy, fulfillment, and a feeling of self-worth.

Certainly, caring, (whether it is a mentally understood action or not), is far better than hurting. As there are many people who find internal solace in doing that, as well. But, the root source of caring must be understood if a person ever hopes to come to a clear, highly defined internal understanding of why they do what they do.

Most people never look. They simple do. The good-hearted do good things. That bad-hearted do bad things.

Good is always better than bad. But, even those who do good should understand their motivations for why they do what they do.

So, next time you are patting yourself on the back for having gone out of your way to help someone out, know your motivations. You too were rewarded for your actions.

*　　*　　*
　　　　　　　10/Jun/2017 07:12 AM

Does an itch, itch until it is scratched?

* * *
09/Jun/2017 03:05 PM

There is always better way to do the things you're doing but are you open enough to explore the possibilities?

Killing the Relationship
09/Jun/2017 07:15 AM

Throughout all of our lives each of us desires to do and/or to become something. But, to become what we hope to be, we need training. In virtually all instances, someone needs to show us how to do the something that we want to do. If we listen, we can learn. If we do not, we cannot. This is the crux of why so few people achieve what they hope to accomplish in life. Their ego keeps them from being able to learn from the someone who can teach them.

I often speak about, *"Disciple Consciousness,"* and how it is a necessary element of life if you truly hope to gain the elemental insight necessary to reach advanced levels of understanding. This is the case for spiritual advancement, physical advancement, (for example in the martial arts), onto gaining the necessary knowledge of how to paint, play music, make movies, or do anything else where there is an actual craft involved. The problem is, everyone is so full of themselves that they skip this step. From this, most of the world's populous never achieves what they hope to achieve as they do not possess the fundamental knowledge to reach their higher goals. What kept them from it? Their ego.

Now, I am not saying that you have to bow down before all of those who are your senior, like say in the guru/disciple relationship. But, what you do have to do is to be able to shut your ego-driven mind down long enough to understand that there are people who have walked the path before you and may be able to guide you in how you can achieve your own dream of doing.

In terms of filmmaking, which is obviously a big part of my life, I discussed the fact in my book, *Independent Filmmaking: Secrets of the Craft,* that, *"There can only be One Captain of the Ship."* For if there are too many cooks in the kitchen not only do unnecessary disagreements arise but the vision gets convoluted. And, that is never a good thing.

This, *"Too many cooks in the kitchen,"* has caused many an independent feature film to fail.

This also lends insight into the faulty personality of some people as they quest to live their dream of filmmaking. While they are still a novice, their ego gets involved and they feel like what they think they know should be taking place or that they are somehow being treated unfairly. But, this all goes back to the framework of, *"Disciple Consciousness"* and, *"One Captain of the Ship."* If the novice can't turn their ego off long enough to learn, they will never learn.

In fact, a few times people have come to me formally seeking to learn the craft of Independent Filmmaking and to have me be their introduction into the actual filmmaking process but their ego got in the way, they had a meltdown, and where are they today? They've never made a film. In other cases, people have come to me, they did learn they craft, and they did make a film.

It is important to note that I am using filmmaking as an obvious example. But, this same mindset spans to all realms of life and learning.

From a personal perspective, I was always willing to learn from the people who had something to teach me. Maybe I didn't personally like or appreciate everything that was going on but I turned my ego off. From this, when it was time, I was able to break out on my own and live my own vision. But first, I was the student.

This is an essential element to ponder as you pass through life and come upon new things that you hope to accomplish. Be willing to be the student. Be willing to listen to what someone else has to say. Be egoless enough to learn. For if you are never a student you can never be the master.

* * *
09/Jun/2017 07:14 AM

It is easy to have big opinions when you have never had to prove yourself on the playing field of life.

* * *
09/Jun/2017 07:10 AM

There is the belief that children are resilient, that children are easily adaptable, but that is not true. Children simply possess the enhanced ability to pretend. But, all forced adaptation leads to is a child developing emotional and psychological problems later in their life.

Seeing Yourself Through the Eyes of Other People
08/Jun/2017 07:38 AM

Some people do all that they can to be liked by others. If someone they know likes something, they like it. If someone they know dislikes something, they too dislike it. Though somewhere deep down inside they may have their own opinion, they hide it from others so that they will be liked.

Other people are forceful in what they think and what they feel. From this, they are the ones that shape the mind of the weak who are too busy seeking acceptance to express what they truly feel. They are also the ones who attract very few close relationships as they drive everyone away by their pig headedness.

Most everyone else falls somewhere in between these two extremes.

Each of us sees the world the way we see the world. Some of us are more outspoken about how we perceive life, while other are most passive in their opinion. Whatever the case, inside each of us we see what we see, we feel what we feel, and we think what we think we know. Whether what we think that we know is right or wrong is almost unimportant as it is what we feel and that is what we base our life choices upon. This is especially the case when it comes to people. We think we know who people are. We think we know what other people think. But, for the most part, unless you truly-truly know a person, your opinion is a guess at best. If you truly think you know a person, the probability is you are far off base when it comes to truly understanding what makes their mind work and what is the motivating factor for them doing what they do.

I recently flashed back to a memory from high school. This memory reminded me of the first time that I actually experienced someone attempting to describe who and what I was. I was in tenth grade and I was invited to a small gathering at a female friend's nearby apartment. We were sitting around doing what teenagers do and someone came up with the bright idea that we should each describe one another the way we think that they are. In a group therapy session this may have been fine, but man, did that exercise go wrong. The host got very pissed at the way people described her. Me, I never really cared what people thought about me, but what struck me was the way a very close friend of mine described me. He was totally off base. I realized, we hung out all the time, and he didn't know me at all. And, that's the thing about life, even the people who are close to you may not truly understand you. Then, there are all the other people out there who don't personally know you at all and yet they are casting all kinds of judgments about you. Welcome to life…

As someone who has been in the public eye for a quite awhile I have heard people come to all kinds of conclusions about me. Most of them are far-far out in left field. Yet, that is what they believe. From this, that is what they speak. For me, I find it interesting to view how other people see me. This, even when they are totally wrong. It provides me with a microscope into human psychology and how certain people project their own shortcomings onto other people. For almost universally, the people who assume they know who I am or why I do what I do project their own insecurities into the equation. This is psychology 101. This is simply what certain people do.

On the other side of the coin there have been people who have used the idealized image of Scott Shaw and what Scott Shaw supposedly does as a source for parody. There was a filmmaking team, at a Midwestern university, about ten years who did a whole mockumentary on Zen Filmmaking using an actor portraying me as the primary character.

I had never met or spoken with any of them. The only contact I had, on any level, was when one of the participants, prior to doing the shoot, (and, of course, not telling me anything about it), contacted me via Myspace and asked about where I got the Chupacabra costume. When I told him that it was professionally created and it was stupid expensive that was the last I heard. Later, somebody told me that the series was up on YouTube. You can find a link to it on my YouTube page. But, that was the first time I heard anything about it. And, I never heard from any of the cast or crew again. I hope they made their filmmaking dreams come true. But, I don't know? I don't even know their names…

Anyway, in that mockumentary they present a certain vision of me and to a lesser degree Donald G. Jackson. It is comedic. But, is it me? No. Was it Don? No.

Again, they never met me, they never spoke to me, yet they used me to present an image of myself and Zen Filmmaking. Good thing I have a sense of humor.

And, this goes to the whole point, people think that they know a person. People think that they know what motivates a person. But, they do not.

A few years after the mockumentary was released somebody contacted me as he was interested in creating a theatrical bio pic film of Don and my life and our Zen Filmmaking. I laughed as I told him it had already been done.

In the martial arts, I have watch as some people have described me and some of the people I actually know very well through a very limited, self-motivated, perspective. Why some martial artists base so much of their life on juvenile criticism, based upon internal self-insecurity, I do not know. But, it has gone on forever and it still goes on. It is ridiculous. All they try to do is cast shade on other practitioners. They should be embracing and respecting one another. But, some do not. I wrote a couple of article on this subject over the past years or so: *The People Who Never Evolve* and *Understanding the Black Belt*.

But again, this all goes back to the fact of people thinking that they know another person when they do not... At least the Zen Filmmaking mockumentary was not based upon a position of mean spiritedness. It was a fun-based portrayal. But, other people just want to throw their own personal opinions around and claim that they are facts—believing they have the right to judge a person. But, do they?

Think about this... Pull somebody you know out of your hat—anybody... What do you think about them? Do you think you truly know them? Look deeper into that concept. Do you really know them or do you just think that you know them?

Do they think that they know you? If they were to describe you, the way my teenage friends and I did all those years ago, how right about you would they be?

In fact, sit down and have a comparison session with that person. Have them describe you and then you describe them. How right where they in describing you? How right were you? Were their thoughts and perceptions correct or false? Were your thoughts and perceptions correct or false? And, what did you not reveal to them? What will they never know about you? What will you never know about them?

Life is complex. Personalities are complex. People are who they are to the world, then they are who they are to their friends and lovers, and then they are who they are only in their own inner mind. You can free yourself by being only the Whole You all the time. But, that is almost an impossible feat as you have to take other people into consideration in all that you say and/or do. Moreover, instead of thinking you know another person, instead of judging them verbally or in your mind, simply let them be perfect in their own space—whatever that space may be. From this, you can focus on your own evolution of consciousness and not waste time thinking about what you think about others that is probably wrong anyway.

The Basketball Syndrome
07/Jun/2017 07:58 AM

When you were a kid playing basketball did you ever dream of becoming a professional basketball player? And, I use basketball as an example. It could be baseball, football, soccer, hockey, you name it... But, when you were a kid playing a sport did you ever envision yourself becoming one of the sport's elite? What did you do about it? Did you only dream or did you actually try?

In life, most people dream about becoming something but few people ever pursue the pathway to its achievement. For example in sports, perhaps you really loved one specific game and you played it all the time. When you got to school did you pursue your dream of playing the game within the confines of the more defined realms of sports; i.e.; training the way a coach wanted you to train, following the rules of the game, and become a true part of a team?

Most people let go of the formal realms of their dream very quickly when the achievement of that dream requires discipline and focus. And, one of the primary elements of discipline is being told what you are suppose to be doing—especially in the early days of training. Many, refuse to listening, believing that they know more than the trainer—the person who has already proven their worth.

Some people do follow the formalized pathway, however. Did you? Did you play high school ball? Did you still dream of advanced achievement in the sport? Were you good enough to play college ball?

In all aspects of life there are those who are naturally good enough and there are those who may not possess the innate ability of some but, none-the-less, they practice to the degree that they rise up above their own limitations. It's hard work but it is doable. Did you do this?

At each level of life there are those who hold the dream and there are those who pursue the dream. If you look around yourself, you will quickly see the ones who did what it took to do what they truly dreamed of doing in life. And, this goes to all levels of life, not just sports. It extends to the world of business, the arts, the humanities, and the service of others.

Dreaming is easy. It takes no effort. Taking about your dreams is easy as all you have to do is talk. But, doing is very difficult. It takes focused energy, training, and defined achievement.

Who are you? Do you follow the path of working-hard to achieve your dreams or do you just dream?

What you do, how you do it, becomes the definition of your life. What will be the definition of your life?

* * *
07/Jun/2017 07:32 AM

What you do today is what creates your tomorrow.

* * *
07/Jun/2017 07:30 AM

If the next pair of shoes you buy were going to be the last pair of shoes you ever bought what kind of shoes would they be?

Do You Remember the TV Show Punk'd?
06/Jun/2017 04:02 PM

Do you remember the TV show that Ashton Kutcher did on MTV a few years back, *Punk'd?* If you don't, what took place is that he and his team would go around and create these elaborate pranks on celebrities making them think something very serious was taking place when it was, in actuality, nothing but a ruse. Anyway, it felt like that happened to me today.

To tell the story, I was kicking back on the patio having a *Venti Flat White* and eating some of their very tasty popcorn at my local Starbucks this afternoon as I frequently tend to do. And, these Zen Filmmakers had stalked me to the location. …I guess I should be more secretive about what I do and where I do it but in this modern day and age it is pretty easy to find out anything about anybody unless they are totally off the grid, which I obviously am not.

Anyway, I noticed a couple of young guys going and sitting down behind me. Didn't really think much of it. There's a high school nearby and that Starbucks often attracts many a student after school. A few minutes later this young guy walks up, pulls out a chair, and sits down at my table. He then went into this whole scene about sharing a drink out of this bottle of ranch dressing he had. He took a drink and offered it to me. He was very convincing. Great actor! Never lost character. Personally, I initially assumed that he had eaten some acid and was just tripping. As I have seen many a person do many a strange thing while on acid. But, a few minutes into it, he extends his hand to shake mine. His friends step in and reveal who and what they are. I loved it! Great job!

They had filmed the scene from behind my head and they asked me if they could do the turn around shot and get my reaction. For obvious reasons I said, *"No,"* and explained there is a number of reasons why I couldn't do that. But, I totally loved what they did! True Zen Filmmaking in its purist form!

If they hadn't been so young, I would have suggested that we go out and make an entire film together. But, in terms of legality, it gets really touchy when you work with someone under the age of eighteen.

But, it's great to witness the craft of Zen Filmmaking moving on, growing, expanding, and encountering new interpretations. Rock on guys! You are great!

Martial Law
05/Jun/2017 03:16 PM

Martial Law was recently imposed in parts of the Philippines which set me to thinking… I once starred in a movie called, *Martial Law*. It was shot in the Philippines. I don't know whatever became of that movie as I never saw it. Though I am sure that it cost a lot of money to film as not only did they fly all of the main actors from the States but it was filmed on 35mm film. And yes, I know, this title has been used for a number of films. But, the one I was in, I don't know what happened to it?

For those of you who may not know, there are a lot of films that are completed and then get lost in *Hollywood Never-Never-Land*. There are all kinds of reasons for this. It's just a fact of life in the film industry. Anyway, back to the point of this blog…

If we look at what Martial Law actually is, it is the powers-that-be taking control over a country and locking it down for the (at least so-called) benefit of the people. I personally witnessed a small example of this during the '65 Watts Riots and once when I was in Burma in there was a military coup and they pretty much shut down the entire country.

The thing is, it is true, most people do not want chaos or damage brought into their life. They want to live a peaceful, productive existence. They do not want to be forced to be, *"Human shields,"* they don't want to be told what to believe, how they must dress, and what they must do when someone else wants them to do it. Currently, throughout the world, however, there are regions where forced conduct is being unleashed with a vengeance, and this is not good. Martial Law is simply another form of this but it is simply called by a different named and claimed to be instigated by a different set of circumstances.

But, think about this, how much of human history has been dominated by this style of forced behavior. The fact is, it is everywhere—all the time. Ask yourself, do you do exactly what you want to do when you want to do it? Probably not. The fact is, yes, certain cultures are far more free than others but we are all dominated by what is expected of us. If we veer too far away from what is expected than we are ostracized; maybe even institutionalized. Yet, rebellion goes on all the time but it is not always good?

Whenever someone voices an opinion there will be those with a differing opinion. If those with a differing opinion are in the position of power, then there may be undesired repercussions coming in the direction of the person who spoke.

Here is the point that we find all elements of human behavior are motivated by one primary principal. That principal is, either the lack there of or the advanced understanding of discretion. Because how you behave and what you say is a choice. Sure, you may feel you are right—sure, you may feel that you have the right to say what you feel and do what you want to do, but if you do not look to the wide spanning consequences of your words and actions then you are locked into a mindset of selfishness and that is never a good place to operate from. That is the place where all problems are born.

At the source of all accepted, verses unacceptable behavior, is a person's own ability to view them self and the variables that make up their life from a realistic perspective. With this as a basis, it can be understood that the conscious individual travels through life thinking about others before only thinking about themselves. They ponder what other people are thinking, what other people are feeling, what other people are desiring, and most importantly what will occur to other people if they say or do anything. For example, to return to the example of the Philippines, when the new president came to power he promised to get rid of the wide spanning drug problem the country possesses. To do this, he went after the drug dealers.

Throughout the world, drugs and drug addiction is a major problem. It causes many people to do many bad things. But, who is the source of the drug problem? At least on the interpersonal level, it is the drug dealer. Do drug dealers do what they do to help people? No. They do what they do to make money, get what they want, and help themselves. Have you ever known a drug dealer? I have. The first thing they do when they meet you is to try to give you drugs for free. Why? Because they want to develop a new customer.

The fact is, no matter how you slice it, recreational drugs are not good. Sure, they may provide you with an altered state of consciousness. But, they cause so many problems in the long run of a person's life that the list is unfathomable. Thus, drug dealers, by whatever name or title, are bad people. They are not thinking about the greater good, they are only thinking about themselves. Thus, governments throughout history have gone after them.

And, this is just one example. If a person is motivated by greed and self-motivated desire, then all elements of their life and any life they impact are left in a constant state of turmoil. Thus, the *powers-that-be* take change.

There is no need for laws if you don't do anything illegal. There is no need for the court of public opinion if you don't say or do anything that hurts anybody.

All life emanates from you. All of your life experiences emanate from you. All the things you do; you do by choice, though you may want to deny that fact—especially if something that you do eventually causes you to feel pain.

A good life is about doing good things. A bad life is defined by saying and doing bad things and then perhaps making excuses or telling lies to cover up the truth of what you have done.

Who are you? What do you have to show for living the life you have chosen to live? How will you be remembered?

The essence of all society is based in the actions taken by one person. All actions are a choice. What choice are you going to make and what wide spanning implications will that choice create?

The actions that affect everyone begin with one person.

* * *
04/Jun/2017 07:35 AM

Who are the people in your dreams?

How You See You Verses How the World Sees You
03/Jun/2017 03:51 PM

When each of us looks in the mirror we see who we believe that we are. The obvious factors of this vision are defined by our race, our gender, our height, our weight, the color or our hair, and the color our eyes. Then, what we see is defined by the style of life that we emulate. This is where hair styles and clothing styles come into play. We are defined by a combination of what we were born to be and what we choose to be. From this, we present ourselves to the world.

When we young, generally in our late adolescence and early adulthood, the style of culture that we wish to portray is most pronounced. This is the period of life when we wish to project the point of culture or subculture that we are most drawn to. This period of life is generally when we are the most, (for lack of a better term), *"Stylish."* Commonly, however, this level of enhanced style quickly fades. As I have long stated, pretty much by the time a person reaches their mid-twenties all semblance of a uniqueness of style has been lost as the person drifts into the mainstream. This is not bad or good this is simply the way it is.

Every now and then, however, you bump into one of those people who holds fast to the uniqueness of their style and the world be damned. For example, there is this guy who lives in my neighbor that I see either walking or sitting on a bus bench every now and then. I would guess him to be in his early forties. He has long brown hair and is clean shaven. He always wears tight black jeans tucked into his cowboy boots and one of those leather hats that were developed in the Nazi movement and brought into modern society via 70s gay culture and later via Rob Halford of the band *Judas Priest*. When it is warmer he wears a sleeveless leather jacket. When it is cooler he wears one of those long, leather military overcoats, also brought into remembrance via Nazi culture. He always carries a cane but does not use it to walk. I would guess, where this man's mind lives is not on the same plane of reality as most of us. Or, is it?

Obviously, this individual has a highly defined vision of himself. I would guess, rock star. But, I could be wrong. Whatever it is, whomever he sees himself to be, he emphatically projects that vision to the world. Is this bad? Not really. If he can find a method to support himself while living this illustrated lifestyle, then however he looks is unimportant.

Most people, however, change so that they can blend in. They hope to live a fruitful life and to do so they need to walk a fairly narrow pathway so that they will fit in and be able to earn their wages.

Times change. Culture changes. Once upon a time if a person had long hair they were totally ostracized. I remember how the police would stop me all the time simply because I had long hair. In the late 1960s and 1970s people would yell, *"Faggot,"* at my friends and I as they drove by—restaurants would not serve us. Just look to movies *Easy Rider* or *Electric Glide in Blue* to see what when on. Now, few people ever think of this factor. Yet, a person's hair style is used in defining who or what they are just as how a person is dressed. From this, a consistency of culture is born.

I remember when the punk rock movement happened in the late 1970s. Though in its first wave everyone still had long hair but then that changed and the hair style became short. From this, all of the people who followed that trend were able to easily find a job as many places would not hire someone with long hair. Though punks were able to blend into the norm, that did not make them one of the norm. Thus, outward projection is not the defining factor of who a person truly is on the inside. And, this is where the complications arise. Are you who you see yourself to be or are you a defined projection of what the world wants you to be?

Luckily, at least in the West and in the enlightened East, a person can be pretty much be whomever they want to be. They can project the style of themselves that they envision with little detriment associated with their life. But, look around you—look in the mirror, are you the person you see in your mind's eye or are you defined by what society wants you to be? The fact is, most people follow the norm.

This is a complicated paradigm. Times change but, in essence, people remain the same. They choose to live their life via a means of seeking acceptance instead of charting a new course of expression, not only for themselves, but in all levels of human activity. Most people seek sameness.

Normal is easy. You run into very few roadblocks if you are normal. But, normal is also boring. It is expected.

Ultimately, who you become in life is defined by what you see in your mind, how you want to be seen by the world, and what the world forces you to become. If you do not think about who and what you are becoming, you are not defined by yourself—you are defined by the some abstract something out-there. If you are living only in your own mind, like the aforementioned person in my neighbor, then you may be true to yourself but you may also be viewed as if you are wearing a costume en route to a Halloween party.

It's a fine line… Who you truly are verses who you are expected to become.

Your life can be art but the artist always pays the highest price for their living the art.

The Things You Shouldn't Do
or Free Speech vs. Hate Speech
01/Jun/2017 09:25 AM

In our currently political climate, here in the United States, everybody has seemingly gotten very vocal about our new and current president. As most people are locked into the mindset of their moment, they believe this is a new style of discourse. It is not. If you look to history, you will see that satisfaction verse dissatisfaction have butted heads throughout our country's evolution. In some cases, this was a subtle form of combat, similar to what took place with our previous president. At other times, it was more pronounced. Now, in the age of instant information and the internet, many voices are screaming out both pro and con.

This being said, how you present your opinion is paramount to how your opinion is interpreted. If you are screaming what you believe nobody wants to listen to you as it hurts their ears.

For example, the comedian who just released a photo of her holding a reproduction of the blooded, cut off head of our current president. It was photographed by a photographer who is known for taking controversial photographs. Perhaps in a different situation, at a time when the man was not our president, this may have been seen as art and/or a social or political commentary. But, whether you agree with the outcome of the election or not, the man is our president. As he is our president, there is a way that is acceptable to present your disfavor and there is a way it should not be presented. Thus, the comedian lost her job at CNN, etc...

Your life is really defined by how you encounter life. Again, in this age of instant information and the internet people feel like they can say or do anything. Primarily they feel this way because they are a No-Thing out there in cyberspace hidden by a screen name that means nothing. At least in the case of the comedian and the photographer they owned who they are and what they are saying. There is something very respectable in that presentation. But again, it goes back to who you are saying what about.

Similarly, there was an entire crew of television talk show personality and various levels of stars who claimed they would leave the U.S. if this man was elected president. They are all still here. So, what does that say about their conviction and, in fact, what does that say about their word?

We all like what we like and we all don't like what we don't like. I say this over and over again. That is natural. Everybody has an opinion. But, just because you have an opinion that does not mean that your opinion is absolutely right. It simply means that it is your opinion. This is one of the biggest mistakes that many people make as they travel through life. Many think that what they believe is right and that everyone else should believe the same way as they do. From this mindset, all kinds of conflict is given birth to.

Moreover, how much of what you like and what you don't like can you truly explain the motivational reason for? For the people who like our current president, why do you like him? For the people who do not, why do you dislike him? This same formula goes to all levels of life. Why do you like what you like and why do you dislike what you dislike? Moreover, what caused you to like what you like and dislike what you dislike? In other words, do you really know yourself? Do you study how you became the person you have become? Do you know why you do what you do when you do it based upon what you believe you like or what you believe you dislike?

How you express what you like or what you dislike sets the stage for how other people will either come to respect or dislike the person that you are. The main thing is that, yes, we all have our opinions but do you express them in a conscious and positive manner? Do you allow room for other people to possess their opinions, as well? Do you express them in a way that does not send out negative messaging—promoting negative thoughts and even negative actions?

To be a conscious individual, you really need to be able to step outside of whatever emotion you are feeling towards a person that you like or dislike and realize that they too are a human being. If they were not already in an elevated position compared to you, you would probably not even be thinking about them, discussing them, or wishing to get your onion about them heard.

The thing is, we all need to respect everyone—even the people we do not agree with or do not like. For if all you do is unleash negativity via criticism or whatever other method, then your entire life becomes nothing more than a life defined by your focus on someone or something else out there.

No matter where you find yourself in your life, in whatever political or cultural climate, be whole onto yourself. Know why you think what you think, know why you feel what you feel, know why you do what you do, and care about the other person more than you care about yourself. This is right way to live life. This is how you make a positive contribution to life.

Don't hurt, only help.

What! We're Not Friends Anymore?
31/May/2017 05:08 PM

    I have always found social media to be a strange beast. There are all of these people out there that you do not know but you become so-called friends with them. Some of these people spill their whole life story onto social media. They tell all of these people, that they do not even know, truly intimate details about themselves. This is especially the case when they are going through something traumatic like a break-up or something. But, for the most part, nobody really knows any of the people that they are passing this personal information along to. You may communicate with them via comments and even messaging BUT YOU DO NOT REALLY KNOW THEM!

    There was a time in the not too distant past when the social media site Myspace really served a purpose. I really liked Myspace back in the back when. I mean, yeah, it was the same, you didn't really know the people you were communicating with, but everyone was on it. There would rarely be a night of the week that I was not put on someone guest list to go and see their band perform or to go to their night club. And, everyone invited me to the screening of their films via that site. Sometimes when I needed to cast a movie or find a location for filming, I would post a notice on Myspace. Because of Myspace I got to work with some really cool people via that site that I would have never met otherwise. When I had lost track of a cast or crew member, and I needed them for a movie, I could always find them on Myspace. In fact, if you watch the first season of the HBO show Silicon Valley, in their opening credits, Myspace was still viable enough to be seen in the animated overpass. But, the fact is, by then, what was once the true Myspace was long gone.

    Moreover, a lot of people got really internet famous via Myspace. I wrote a piece about that in a previous blog a while back. It was a great site! Though it is still up, what it has changed into, is nowhere near the same. I do not know why they threw away their business model? Bad move! For those of you who weren't there, back when, you will simply have to take my word for it. But, it was great!

Facebook has never become what Myspace was. Though it is certainly the main media go to site of the day.

In some ways, Facebook serves a similar purpose as Myspace did. People post stuff, some tell their life story, and stuff like that. Me, not so much... Sure, I'm on there. It's a fun place to check out some of the various news and cultural feeds around the world and to occasionally see what's going on with someone I actually (in the real world) know. Some people even friend me. All good... Though if you want to see what's actually up with me, it's far better to check out scottshaw.com—though you can certainly message me on Facebook and if you are not an asshole I will probably respond.

An interesting thing I noticed recently was that this one person had friended me awhile back. They were a friend of a friend. At one point they inquired and I happily gave them some extended information about working in the film business. They asked. I answered. No problem... Then, our new president got elected and a lot of people took to the streets. This is the United States of America you can do that... In reference to that, I did write a blog about how some of the people who are protesting are not legally in this country and are not U.S. citizen. I do have a bit of problem with that as they tend to be the ones causing all the damage. And damage, on any level, is never a good thing! Anyway, I guess this girl took that blog as a personal insult, though it was not intended that way. She is one of those people who has long been legally living in this country but has never become a U.S. citizen, though she easily could have done so. In my mind, the fault is hers. If you want to be here, be here. If you want to protest, first become one of us. Yet, she was out there protesting, causing havoc, breaking stuff, telling her story on Facebook, and making excuses why she hasn't become a U.S. citizen. Though I didn't even think about her when I wrote the blog, I guess she thought about me…

Anyway, I looked as I was going to offer her a role in an upcoming movie and I thought I would contact her via Facebook. …But, I noticed that we're not friends anymore.

Oh well… Nothing lost, nothing gained… ☺

The United States of America, this is a great place! But, if you're going to be here, be here. Be one of us.

Nature, Conflict, and Your Reaction to the Reaction
30/May/2017 07:14 AM

As we are in the midst of Spring here in Cali, every morning as soon as the first light hits the horizon there is this symphony of bird song permeating the air. They all sing. As the light grows stronger the chirping slowly subsides until it becomes just the more common song off in the distance. The sounds are great.

There is this field out in front of where I live. For whatever reason feral cats always seem to find their way there and make it their home. How or why, I do not know. Though Animal Control frequently picks them up, a new and different cat culture always seems to appear. Recently, I began hearing these two cats periodically meowing very loudly. At first, I though they were just having sex. But then one day I looked. It was two cats sitting right in front of each other screeching at one another. *"I hate you!" "No, I hate you more!"*

Sometimes, I will grab my binoculars and watch them. They sit there for a long time staring each other down, non-stop meowing at one another. They never fight. They just meow. Then, something will distract one or the other of them and they move along. They move along until the come back and do it again. Very interesting…

As someone who has had a number of cats over the years, I have watched as each one has a very unique personality. Some love each other. They sleep together, play together, fight together—they are soul mates. Then, when one eventually passes away the other is so heart broken they die soon after. Other cats tolerate each other. Some even dislike one another. But, because they are living in the same space they make it work.

Nature is this great sphere of reality. It is really beautiful if you take the time to watch it unfold and look and listen to what it has to offer. People on the other hand, they get all locked up in their heads; being unhappy and unfulfilled which equals being depressed and all other kinds of less than ideal reactive emotions. But, why are people unhappy and unfulfilled? They are unhappy and unfulfilled because they refuse to let themselves be whole onto themselves. They refuse to accept their reality and make the best of it. From this is born a person defined by judgment, critical thought, and negative though patterns which lead to a life defined by lack of fulfillment and unhappiness.

How do you live your life? Are you locked in your own head projecting whatever negativity you may be feeling onto others? How about when you are happy, doing something you like, then what? What do those moments cause you to do?

If all you do is embrace what you don't have, what you are not, what you don't like, and who you don't like, then you are trapped into the world of those two cats staring at each other, screaming your displeasure, and your life wastes away into nothing but misplaced anger.

Move on. Let go of hate, anger, and dissatisfaction. Stop casting your negative self-projections outwards. Accept who and what you are—accept who and what everyone else is, and be happy within yourself.

The Dojang Experience
29/May/2017 08:02 AM

Here is an article I wrote and published in the first collection of writings for the Scott Shaw Zen Blog in probably 2011. You can also find it in my first blog based book, <u>Scribbles on the Restroom Wall</u>. I was just thinking about this article so I thought I would repost it. Enjoy...

The Korean term, *"Dojang,"* is used to describe a martial art training facility. The Japanese term, *"Dojo,"* is perhaps the more commonly known word, used to describe the same training space.

Most people have the belief that a dojang is some sort of scared space where only the higher learning of the martial arts is transacted. For me, this was amusingly not the case.

My first martial art training began when I was six. Though, in fact, I had always possessed a rudimentary understanding of the martial and fighting arts as my father earned his black belt during World War II and my uncle had been a professional boxer prior to World War II.

My first teacher was a Korean born Hapkido black belt. This man was probably one of the first Hapkido black belts to immigrate to the U.S. Though he never owned a formal school, he was one of the first people, I know of, to have taught Hapkido in the U.S.; though he referred to it by one of its earlier names, Ho Shin Moo Do. Me, as a six-year-old, I just thought I was studying Karate.

This man made his living as a gardener and he trained a group of young South Korean student in his back yard. As he was a friend of my father's, I was allowed to train with them.

I always remember how nicely groomed his yard was. He had a couple of nicely trimmed trees and nice flowers and plants lined his fence. I mean, he was a gardener after all...

The man would train the five or six of us, as he walked around with a bamboo staff to smack us with, if we did something wrong, and a cigarette hanging out of his mouth. I didn't really think that much about it as both of my parents smoked. In fact, even my dentist, who was also Asian, used to sit overlooking his dentist chair, with a cigarette burning behind him, as he examined my teeth. It was obviously a different era. ☺

After earning my black belt, I eventually went to a couple different dojangs through my teenage years, as we moved around the L.A. area more than a little bit. All were operated by Korean born teachers. And, though they didn't walk around the training floor smoking as they taught their classes, they all would sit at their desk or in their waiting room, smoking.

By the time I was twenty-one, I was helping a newly arrived Korean master I had met in Seoul establish his business. I taught virtually all of the classes for him for years. Though he had a No Smoking sign behind his desk, he constantly smoked in the dojang. Perhaps even more interesting is the fact that each day he would have his friends come by and they would go out to the central dojang floor, sit there smoking, drinking, and playing Ma Jak. Ma Jak is more commonly know as Mahjong. Ma Jak is a Korean gambling game that they would play all day.

If you have ever watched Koreans playing this game, it is quite a site. They get all excited as they yell and scream as they toss down the small tiles, (which are kind of like dominos), and are used to win or lose the game.

He was actually one of my two most influential teachers. He was already in forties when I met him but was still a great physical technician. For those non-martial artists out there who may not be aware of this, by the time you reach your forties, having practiced the martial arts for your entire life, your body is most commonly rapidly breaking down, maybe even already trashed, due to all of the harsh training that goes hand-in-hand with the martial arts. But, he could still fly through the air quite gracefully.

We became good friends. He and I would go out and get drunk at the Korean hostess bars in Koreatown, at strips clubs, and occasionally partake of other substances. But, those are other stories…

One thing that most people probably don't understand is that, even though most South Korean men are avid churchgoers, they are very old school. They, like I, judge a man by how much he can drink. Though I was only twenty-one when I first began working with this man, I had already, long ago, developed the ability to be able to drink round-for-round with the best of 'em. So, I was readily accepted into their community. Few non-Koreans are ever let inside this world.

Eventually, he got remarried, stopped the partying, and several years later, he and I had a major falling out. I never saw him again. But, that's fine. "Falling out," lets you move away from one situation and chart out new territories.

But, I always fondly remember his school and how for the years I worked with him, he and his friends would sit around the training floor, smoking and playing Ma Jak each day as they yelled while they threw down the tile pieces and screamed at each other.

Dojangs, they are not always what they seem. ☺

When the New Has Become Old
28/May/2017 07:52 AM

Have you ever had the experience where you all of sudden remember something that you used to do—you liked to do it, but you no longer do it anymore? You may not even remember why you stopped doing it, but your doing it was lost somewhere in your past.

Life is process of human evolution. Most of that evolution is forced upon us. We are told to go to school. We are told we need a job. We have to eat, we have to live, so we have to work to survive. Within this sphere of reality much of what we do and the way we do it is dictated to us. Though there may be specific patterns that we individually develop to do what we do, much of our course of life action is set in stone.

Then, on a personal level, there are those things that we decide that we like to do. There are those things that feel good, so we do them. In this space, we are allowed to individually evolve and create our own applications to make things feel right. We do them, the way we want to do them, and we do them as long as we can.

In each of the aforementioned cases, there is the way we do and, for most, the way we do what we do changes very little throughout a lifetime. This is what may be termed, *"Life stagnation."* But, most people never even ponder how they do what they do, they never experiment with new ways of doing, they just what they do the way they do it.

Somewhere, in each of our lives, things and situations change. For those who have an observant mind, they realize that our mind, our body, our perception of reality, our understanding of suchness changes. We each come to new terms with and for specific actions. From this, many things are let go of as we pass though our existence. Though, in some cases, we may not want to let them go—times and life change and we must let go.

Then, there are those things that we simply forgot about doing. We forgot how we used to do them. We forgot, until that small inkling of a memory emerges and we are reminded. Reminded, of how what we used to do felt good, did good, was good. Good… But, that doing is now gone. Gone, but we never saw it leaving us. We never took notice of its exit.

How much of your doing has passed without a notice? How much of how you used to do things has been replaced with the necessary, the ordinary, the easier, and/or the forgettable?

Life is your pathway. This life is all you have. How you encounter this life is all that you can remember. If you forget the way you used to do things, what is left? What then remains is nothing more than a life forgotten.

* * *

28/May/2017 07:44 AM

Everybody wants to talk about what someone else has done so they don't have to look at their own faults and flaws.

The World of Good and Bad
27/May/2017 06:15 PM

We live in a world where there are two elements: good and bad. Though people try to make excuse for doing bad things, there is no level of variance within these two factors. There is only good and there is only bad.

People know what is good and what is bad.

Some people actually attempt to define their life by doing only good things. Other people know what is bad but they justify their actions to themselves and to others. They make excuses to themselves for doing what they know is not right.

If you do not actually know what is good and what is bad you are lost.

If you are not listening to your inner voice when it is telling you what you are about to do is bad, then you are in denial.

If you choose to do bad things and justify your actions, what do you think you will ultimately encounter in life? A justification is simply a lie defined by different logic.

There is good and there is bad. Think about this before you choose to do anything.

* * *

27/May/2017 06:14 PM

If you do something good for someone and they don't know that you did it does it diminish the goodness of the deed?

If you do something bad to someone and they don't know that you did it does it diminish the evilness of the deed?

You Need to be Ready for the Buddha to Arrive
27/May/2017 07:32 AM

Most people operate their lives from the perspective that the future will take care of itself. They do not think, nor do they plan for what comes ahead. They certainly do not plan for their ultimate demise. From this, they do not allow themselves to live and encounter a life lived by the definition of conscience consciousness. They also do not prepare themselves and their loved ones for their final passage from this life; i.e. death. Most people do what they do until they can do it no longer. This is the definition of an unconscious life.

As I often detail, most people are good people. They do not intentionally do bad things. They do not hurt, steal, or intentionally damage the lives of others. Their life is not defined by a long list of rationalizations and justifications for the life they live and what they do in the life they live. They simply go to school, go to work, maybe go to church, and they do the best they can to take care of their families. They do what they do until they do it no longer.

I won't even go into the people who do bad, self-motivated, things because they are simply bad people. They will eventually get what they deserve. But, the problem with living your life from a lack of perspective—with a loss of conscience interaction with your life and the universe is that your life goes by, nothing was consciously achieved, and when you come to the point of your death you leave this life not a better place and quite often your family in chaos.

In some way I feel I was blessed in that I observed the recurrence of family deaths early in my life. Whether it was a close family member's unexpectedly passing or a young family members dying in war, what comes next is what comes to define the life that person lived. As I have passed through my own life I have also witnessed how some people pass from their existence very consciously while others did not. Those who encountered life and death consciously left those who loved them sad but aware and in control. Those who who lived a life of chaos left the lives of those who loved them in chaos.

Your life (everybody's life) always comes do down to the definition of who are you? What have you done? Who have you done what to? And, what service, or lack thereof, did you provide to this life space.

Most people make excuses throughout their life for doing what they do. *"I like it." "I want it." "It makes me happy." "This is how I make my living." "I had a bad childhood so I do this because…" "I like to collect things so I'm a hoarder." "I have mental issues." "People don't care about me so I don't care about people,"* And, the list goes on and on. But, all an excuse ever can be is an excuse. If you are not doing what you are doing from a position of prescribed consciousness, hurting no one, than what does that say about you?

Most people do not want to look at themselves. They do not wish to study who they truly are and why. Thus, they make excuses.

If you define your life by a never ending list of justifications and excuses for who you are, what you are doing, and why you are doing it, all you do, throughout your life, is hurt other people and create unnecessary chaos. This is not a life defined by conscience consciousness.

How many people have you known who are doing something bad or wrong and once they are either caught or confronted with this fact get mad at the person they are doing this bad thing to? That is the ideal definition of a life lived via unconscious chaos.

People who follow the spiritual path—a true spiritual path not some negative self-involved nonsense, do so as an understood means to make not only themselves but this life place a better space. They strive to remain conscious. They think of others first. They set up their lives to have a formalized structure of consciously doing good things and of intentionally hurting no one.

Where is your life at? How do you encounter life? Are you hurting or are you helping? If you are somewhere in-between, defined by rationalizations and justifications, you are hurting.

If you care enough to care, you really need to constantly study your life because your unexpected passing could occur at any moment. If you hope to be remembered in a positive fashion, if you hope to have made a positive contribution to life, you need to operate from a place of refined conscience consciousness.

Who are you? How are you defined by others? If you don't care, that is the ultimate definition of your life.

Be more and care. Caring is defined by consciously caring about the impact you are having. Care about others before you care about yourself and everything in this life becomes better.

Live a conscience life and invoke no chaos. Then, when the Buddha comes knocking, you can greet him and happily invite him in.

*   *   *
24/May/2017 04:53 PM

When was the last time that you gave somebody something? Not somebody you know. Not somebody you love. Just somebody you decided to give something to.

Who Am I to Judge?
AKA How Many Books Do You Have in the Library of Congress?
24/May/2017 12:58 PM

Do you remember a couple of years ago when the band U2 released their the new album and due to their relationship with Apple it was automatically uploaded to the iTunes app on every iPhone? A lot of people got very upset. So, U2 did this whole onscreen apology thing. I always wondered why they did that. Just let it go. It will be forgotten. Do you even remember that occurrence?

Now, I have never really been a fan of U2's music. But, that's just me. They have proven their worth. I mean they have been superstars forever. They have millions of fans. Yet, people judge them... But, how can anyone do that?

It always strikes me as strange why people are so judgmental. We all like what we like and we don't like what we don't like. It should be left at that. But some, they are so vocal.

Me, wherever somebody expresses misdirected criticism my direction, (to my face), my question/statement always is, *"How many books do you have in the Library of Congress? Because, I have several."*

In any case, I was at a party thrown in honor of U2 last night as they just played two nights at the Rose Bowl over the weekend. It was one of those total Hollywood galas with stars and want-be stars everywhere. Me, I have never really been a fan of parties. I usually just grab a glass (or bottle) of wine and go and sit in the corner and watch the unravelings. That's what I did last night. I watched as everyone wanted their selfies with Bono and The Edge and/or whatever other star or Hollywood big wig they thought was approachable. I always take terrible selfies so I rarely bother. But, as I sat there, I listened to this one couple totally bagging on U2. *"They're too old. They are like an oldies band doing cover songs of their own music and so on..."* But then, awhile later, I saw that couple licking the feet of Bono trying to catch a photo op.

This is life. This is particularly the life of Hollywood. But, life is the same everywhere. People wish they could be the people they criticize. People wish they had achieved what the people they criticize have achieved. People want whatever it is the people they criticize have to rub off on them.

Life is one of those uncharitable courses. For whenever reason, some people rise up while others do not. Maybe it's luck. Maybe it's karma. Maybe it's magic. Or, maybe it's sheer force of will and hard work—that is my belief. But, whatever it is, if all you do is talk and criticize, and try to take a selfie with Bono in the background, your life will never equal anything.

Letters as a Literary Exercise
24/May/2017 09:11 AM

If you're interesting in art or literature or anything like, and the people who create it, you will find that there are numerous books, based on the letters that these creators wrote to other people. In some ways, I always found that this was a bit of an invasion of privacy. …That people who knew nothing about the true backstories of these individuals were peering into their life. On the other hand, it also provides a unique microscope into the mind of the people who wrote these letters. Overall, as these books are almost always based on the correspondence of one person, they do provide interesting insight into the mind of that person.

There was a time in my life when I read and collected an enormous amount of books. At that time, I did read a number of these letter-based books based around the letters composed by the authors and artists I appreciated.

I don't know if it was so much due to that influence or simply at that point in history people tended to exchange handwritten letters but I too spent a lot of time communicating with people via pen on paper. Of course, this was before e-mail. And, even though I was one of the very early participants of what later became known as the internet, most people did not have a personal computer at that point in history. So, writing letters was the only true form of distant communication.

Anyway, I wrote and received a lot of letter. And yes, I did see it as a literary art form. In many cases, I would send letters in combination with a poem I had written in association with the person. Perhaps I would send a small piece of art work or a drawing within or on the letter. It was a great time for interpersonal (very-personal) communications. As I traveled a lot, I communicated with people, (mostly girls), via letter, all across the globe.

The one thing that I realized back then, during that period of letter communications was, that you communicate with a specific person in a specific fashion. What and how you interact with one person is often times very different than what and how you interact with another. In many cases, you tell a person what you believe that they want to hear via your letters. You present the part of yourself that you want them to see. In other words, when you are communicating, via distance and not in real time, you say things that are based upon a distant reality of projected suchness. When you are one-on-one with a person you tell them immediately what you want and/or how you are feeling. When it may take them a week or more to get your letter, you present a version of desired reality based upon a lack of real time emotions. In other words, you may be telling them what they want to hear or you may be telling them what they don't want to hear but as you are not face-to-face or in real-time communications the reality of emotion is lost via the translation of time.

What I am saying is that lying via snail mail is much easier and/or even more necessary than in the age of instant communication that lives today.

And, this goes to the point and principal of what you read when you are reading the personal communications of someone else. You do not know, you will never know, their true intensions as their true intensions are vailed by what they wanted that other person to believe via a specific letter.

The fact is, much of life is based upon lies. People lie. It is as simple as that. Though they may not choose to call it a lie, everyone does what they do based upon how they want the world to perceive them. Thus, the words they speak, the letters they write, are based upon a perceived and projected reality that may only truly be understood by the author. Though the fact(s) be told, many people are out of touch with their true inner-motivations, they possess no self-control or self-discipline, so what they do is based upon a completely baseless, false reality. So, what are you left with? Written words mean very little.

Somewhere back in the late 90s or early 2000s I came upon my collection of letters that I had received from my correspondence across the globe. With them, I also found copies of some of the letters I had written. Interesting, yes. But, I destroyed them all. It was so freeing. It was such a release. It felt so good to leave the past behind.

Going to the point of all of this, the people who these books of correspondences are based upon, where almost all created after the person had passed away. Thus, the actual composer of these letters had no say in their being published. They had no way to add annotations about what was their mindset at a specific period of time. These books lock these people to a specific point in time. They lock these people to specific words written. Maybe these words were based in true emotion. Maybe they were based in projected emotions. Maybe they were based in lies. Whatever the case, these published words are used to detail the mind and mindset of a specific individual. But, how can that ever be? It is not reality. At best, it is only the reality of a specific moment and specific though pattern, used in association with a specific person. It is not true. It is not real. It is only words written on page. And, these words were stolen by the person or persons who wanted to publish them.

There is only one reality and that is the reality of your now. Yes, your past and what you have done and whom you have done it with, in your past, created your now, but that was then not now. You are only who you are right now. If you lock your life into a time period of the emotions you felt, *"Back then,"* of the person you were, *"Back then,"* you can never be whole in your now. You can never become the new and better you that each new day of life provides you with. Thus, the literary letters of yesterday should not define your today. Destroy your past and you are free.

Be new onto your new day.

You Need a Tool for God
AKA God is a Dangerous Concept
23/May/2017 03:08 PM

I was having breakfast this morning in a restaurant. In front of me sat this elderly man. His wife apparently died yesterday. It was truly touching in that each of the waitresses, who worked in the restaurant, came up to him one by one and each, with total compassion, a couple with tears in their eyes, wished him well. One said, *"God will take care of you."* He and his wife must have been regular customers.

Behind me, sat two men. One was a seeker, the other was a preacher. The preacher exclaimed, *"You need a tool for god. If you want to build a house you go to Home Depot and buy the tools you need. That's the same with building your relationship with god. You get the tools and you go to work for him."* Then, they prayed.

People forever use, *"God,"* as a commodity. ...A thing that you do things for and a thing that will do things for you. But, I have always believed that this is a dangerous belief system. Think about all that bad things that have been done in the name of god and all the people that did those bad things believing it was for god: The Crusaders, The Kamikaze, all the psychos who use god as a reason for them doing what they do, onto all of these people who are currently doing suicide bombings. ...One happened just last night at a concert. These people are told, they are brainwashed into believing, that what they are doing they are doing for god and they will be rewarded for their actions. But, where is that reward? It is somewhere else, in some abstract dimension that is only based in belief. Did the Christians that died during The Crusades go to the same heaven as the Muslims? And, if not, who went where and why?

Belief is a dangerous slope to walk along. It is particularly dangerous if you are using it as a motivating factor to do anything.

A very minor example could be Mother Teresa of Calcutta. I briefly worked with her on two occasions. She helped a lot of people. But, what is not well known here in the Western World is that she was a very controversial figure in India. Why? Because sure, she was providing a great, selfless service, but she was also a Christian attempting to convert the people that she helped to Christianity. Now, this is a small sin if it is a sin at all. She was doing what she was doing for her god but she was requesting a price be paid. Certainly, she set out to intentionally hurt no one. But, did those who converted to Christianity encounter complications from their own Hindu or Muslim families and/or brotherhood due to their converting? And, did anyone take notice or care? We will never know who endured what?

The thing is, a Christian would say, *"Whatever the cost, now they are going to heaven."* But again, where is that heaven? And, what about the obstacles those people were forced to endure in their life due to the promise of that heaven? Sure, it is easy to dismiss anyone else's trials and tribulations and everyone will claim, *"My god is the only true god."* But, if the concept of a new and different god were not introduced to these people none of those complications would have been encountered.

God is an abstract phenomenon. Though the belief in god may provide comfort in times of need it also has been the motivating factor for more of this world's devastations that any other one thing.

You really need to think about god on a much deeper level before you decide to do anything for god, as god is just a promised, abstract concept that lives nowhere but within people's minds.

The Instigator and How The Small Things Set The Big Things Into Motion
22/May/2017 05:28 PM

As I often discuss, I believe that life is the best teacher. As such, I am constantly aware of what is going on around me; studying the way people behave, how they interact with others, and what occurs due to this interaction. Via observance, I believe that we each can not only learn a lot about the play of life but we can also learn a lot about ourselves as we can witness how we react to each life occurrence.

The fact is, what one person decides to do in any moment has the potential to set a whole course of life events into motion. If somebody is doing something good, kind, and positive, good things may occur. If someone is doing stupid, selfish, unkind, unthinking, or negative things, bad things may occur.

Do you ever think about what you are doing before you do it? Do you ever question the possible repercussions of your actions before you take them? Or, do you just do, thinking of nothing and no one?

A very minor situation happened to me today. As it occurred it shook me out of the normalness of life and made me again become the witness to how the actions of others have the potential to set an entire course of events into motion.

I was at a stop light and the light turned green. Before I even had a chance to push down on the gas pedal the guy behind me honks his horn. Normally, all the stupidness of life does is amuse me. But sometimes, just like everyone, the actions another person takes rubs me the wrong way. In any case, I pull away from the light. And, like in the preverbal Fellini movie, the guy who honked at me, a chubby middle-aged white guy with curly hair drives by me in his mini van, with his white poodle hanging out of the window. As he drives by he flips me off. Now, if I was one of those people prone to road rage, that would have really set me off. Luckily, I am pretty much in control of myself. But, did it piss me off? Sure. And, though it could have sent me to pursing the guy, I have long realized that nothing good comes from saying or doing anything negative. Moreover, say I would have kicked the guy's ass. Then what? Then comes the law and the lawsuits and all that. But, what he did and whom he did it to could have had an entirely different outcome. Yet he, as the instigator, started it all.

I think back to a friend I had when I was in 6th grade though junior high. He was one of those people, even at that young of an age, that would instigate people to do all kinds of things. He would instigate but he would never do. Thus, everyone around him would get into trouble. Everyone, except him. Luckily, I was not easily seduced into that world. So, I came out relatively unscathed. But, I watched, even back then, how what he would instigate would set this whole course of events into motion that literally changed some people's entire lives for the worse. And, this style of behavior goes on all around us, all the time.

I lost touch with him but I heard that he passed away in his early forties. Sad, I thought, as we were very good friends for a time. But, I also wondered if he had continued his practice of instigation throughout his lifetime. I guess I will never know.

The thing is, you really need to think about what you are doing and how you are behaving because what you do can set an uncharitable course of events into motion. A course of events that you can never predict where it will end. You really have to think before you do.

Do you think before you do? If you don't, it's time to start.

* * *
22/May/2017 05:27 PM

You are only thinking that because you have nothing better to think about.

Holier Than Thou
22/May/2017 05:07 PM

As we pass through life, I think most people we meet are fairly nice. Sure, everyone has their own unique personality flaws but they are not bad people. Of course, there are also the total nut-jobs out there that each of us will most likely encounter—those people that will mess with our lives, but hopefully those interactions are few and far between.

On the other side of the issue, I think we will all encounter the person who is holier than thou. Though this person has personally accomplished very little in their own life they are the one who speaks the loudest about who or what they do or do not like. But, why do they do this? I guess it is simply based upon insecurity or misdirected anger but I suppose each case is unique.

Having spent most of my life formally involved with the martial arts, (for over fifty years now), I have occasionally interacted with martial artists who hold this holier than thou mindset.

First of all, I must state, that most of the advanced martial artist I have known are very nice people. They work hard on themselves, on teaching what they have learned, and they respect others. There is a small subset, however, that are really focused on misplaced judgment. I always find this curious as the true martial arts are about universal betterment. They are never about judgment. But, some practitioners, somehow, have come to focus on their judgment of others instead of making themselves a better person. This practice particularly erupted with the birth of the internet. Then, nameless, faceless people found a voice—a voice where there would and could be no repercussions.

I have witnessed the evolution of the martial arts in the West. When the marital arts were new to the United

States, the Asian instructor held dominance. As they were from Asia, everyone believed that they must know more. They must be better. This trend has never truly subsided. But, as someone who has personally witnessed a lot of the inner-shenanigans that went on as the modern Asian based martial art systems took hold in American, I can personally say that if you weren't there you will never understand. ...The stories I could tell but won't...

The thing is, once upon a time, a martial art student was certified only by his instructor. As I have often said, I believe this is probably the best and most conscientious method of certification for who knows a student better than their instructor? But then, the mindset changed as the late 70s and early 80s rolled around and some people felt that if a martial artist wasn't certified by a large organization than their certification was somehow not valid and opened to criticism. But again, as someone who personally saw the interworkings of Asian based martial arts organizations, from their inception forward, I can truly say that they are not necessarily the absolute authority. Again, the stories I could tell...

From this era was born many an instructor forming their own organization. I did it too. My organization formed more as a necessity, as at the time—in the late 70s, it was very hard to get certificates from Korea. You pretty much had to go there to get black belt level certification and most students could not afford that journey. But, what did all this equal? All it did was to add new fuel to the fire and provide fodder for those of a judgmental mind to find a reason for criticism.

Here… This goes to the heart of the issue. Who is saying what and why? What all-knowing credential does some person possess that allows them to cast a universal judgment on anybody or anything?

The fact is, those people who are saying negative things are, in fact, less than the people they are criticizing as they are nobodies. What have they accomplished?

As is always the case in life, those of like-mind find one another. Those who are positive and want to be helpful to others find each other and help. Just as those who are negative, judgmental, self-loathing, and insecure find one another and do their damage. This is just the way of life. And, it is essential to note that I have just been using the martial arts as an example as it is an easily established reference point. But, this kind of stuff goes on all around us in every venue: in the film industry, in literature, in sports, in human awareness, and all other formulated disciplines out there.

Now, I can state, *"You should only say and do good, positive, and helpful things."* But, the good and positive people are the only ones who will listen. The others, who embrace negativity, don't want to hear it. They get adrenalized from being critical. It provides them with a sense of power. Though they should be working on themselves, instead they find it easier to focus on something out there that has no true effect on their life.

One can question, *"Why are you doing it?"* But, for a person who embraces this mindset, they will always be able to come up with an answer. You or I may call it a justification but they will believe it to be a right and righteous attitude. So, where does this leave us?

I believe at the heart of any judgment is a person wishing to appear to be more than that person or that thing that they are judging. Think about it, if they did not believe that they were more they would not be casting their judgment at all.

Understanding this, I think this is the first definition that you must examine whenever you hear a person making a judgment call. By understanding them, you understand their motivation, and from this, you can come to your own valid conclusion(s) and not simply believe something that someone else is vainly stating.

As we pass through life, we all meet the holier than thou. As we pass though life, we will all reach our own judgments and conclusions about other people and other things. But, if we can remain conscious, if we can remain open, if we can be secure within ourselves, we will never become lost in the realms of believing that we know more than someone else or falsely believing that we are better than someone else as we are wholly and completely who we are and know that everyone else is simply who and what they are.

Judgment removes everyone from reality. Judgment is only a thought in your mind that you may or may not project to the world. But, the truly conscious individual says nothing about anybody as they understand that no one is more or less than anyone else.

* * *
21/May/2017 07:59 PM

Did something you said or did negatively affect the life of someone yesterday, last month, last year, five years ago, ten years ago? If it did, that is the definition of your life.

People always wonder why they do not achieve what they hope to achieve. But, they never look to themselves as the causation factor for their condition.

Fix what you have done then maybe your life will be repaired.

* * *
21/May/2017 05:05 PM

When you are the one voicing a negative opinion you should really think about your motivation.

The Gift of Non-Giving
21/May/2017 08:01 AM

Have you ever given somebody something and they did not appreciate it? Maybe you really looked hard for something that they wanted and you found it, maybe you spent a lot of money on it, maybe you really went out of your way to do something for them, maybe you took them under your wing and helped them achieving something in their career, maybe you gave them a sacred part of yourself and they took it without a second thought. There are a lot of things one person can give to another person but if what you give is unappreciated then what is anyone left with? The other person has gotten something and you are left with less due to the giving.

Life is a complicated interplay of human personalities and physical actions. We all are who we are. We are who we choose to be. We react how we choose to react. And yes, how you behave in each life situation is a choice. Thus, everything is your fault.

We all do what we do as we pass through life. Some people make conscious choices with focused intent trying to do only good things. Others are not so conscious, however. They do what they do, driven by any number of random personal characteristics. They do but they don't care what they do nor do they care about whom they help or whom they hurt in the process. They simply react.

Taking is easy. That is why so many people are hurt in their giving. The people they give to don't care about the cost to anyone else as long as they receive.

Giving is kindhearted and caring. But, in all giving, there is a personal price that must be paid.

Many people are willing to pay that price. They give and give only attempting to make the life of one person or the entire world better. But, the process of giving is also a process of diminishing. You can only give until you have no more to give. Then you are left barren.

Some people are lucky, they find interactive relationships where there is a constant sense of giving and receiving. Thus, there is an interpersonal flow of replenishment.

The lives of most people are not like that, however. That is one of the key reasons why there is conflict within most personal relationships. People do business. They associate with a person for as long as it serves their purpose: be this in a business setting, a family relationship, or a love connection. They are there as long as the relationship is necessary for them to get what they want. When they are no longer on the receiving end, the relationship is over.

The fact is, some people give so that they will receive. But, this is not giving at all. That is a ruse. This is simply someone finding a new reason to take under the guise of giving.

So, what does this leave us with in life? What can we do when we give but our giving is unappreciated? What can we do when we give until we have nothing left to give? And moreover, what can and should we do when we receive?

At the root of all life is your conscious and caring interaction with all of those you interact with. Again, how you behave throughout your life is your choice. Thus, as in all cases, all life begins with you.

Care. It is as simple as that. Do not expect to receive but when you do care that anyone gave you anything and be appreciative. When you give understand that all people do not live in a space of consciousness. Thus, until you deeply understand the person you are giving to, do not give them anything that will damage your life in the process.

You can give until it hurt but who does that serve? You can take more than you deserve but then what are you left with? You can be appreciative in the gifts you receive and then you will be loved. You can be greedy and hurt those who give to you but then you will be scorned.

Giving is a life choice. Taking is a life choice. But, how you give or how you receive defines you as a human being. Think about this before you give or you take.

* * *

20/May/2017 03:27 PM

How much of your life do you spend accomplishing as opposed to simply doing?

Poetry and The Road of No Return
20/May/2017 07:28 AM

I was kicking around New Delhi in India in '82 and this guy comes up me. He was a relatively young, maybe late twenties, local. He starts a conversation with me but as everyone is on the hustle in India I was reluctant to speak with him. He spoke, telling me how he had recently returned from the U.K. and then he tries to sell me a small chapbook of his poetry. He needed money. He hoped to return to the U.K.

For those of you of a different era and time, a chapbook is a small book of poetry either produced by the poet or a small publishing company in order to get the words of that poet out to the world of those who read poetry. Who reads poetry? Anybody? Anybody?

The chapbook was the standard method used from the late forties through the early nineties until the internet took over the world. Every poet from the now elites of the craft, like Ginsberg and Bukowski, to every other poet had chapbooks created. Me too…

The man only wanted a few rupees so I purchased the book from him. As a person who has always been into reading and writing poetry, I though it may be an interesting addition to my collection. As I left, I realized that he wasn't just another hustler. At that point, I would have spoken to him further, as it sounded like he had lived an interesting life, but I never saw him again.

Anyway, a few years later I watched this very good 1984 TV mini series about India, *The Jewel in the Crown*. There was this one lead character, of East Indian descent, who had been schooled in the U.K., had returned to India, fallen in love with a Caucasian woman, and all was going fine until something really bad happened to her in this man's presence. Like I have always told everyone, India is a violent place. But, at the end of the mini series, you see this man, who had spent the better part of his life trying to get back to the U.K., but could not. You find him living in a small city dwelling, the loud sounds of the city pouring in, with a picture of his one and only true love on the wall. Total tear-jerker. But, this is the thing about life that you must always keep in mind during the living of whatever it is you are living—you may be on a road of no return so you really have to appreciate all you are doing in your moment as your moment may come and then go and it may never return.

I imagine that each of us in our lives have been doing something that we really liked. Maybe this something only lasted for a few moments, maybe a day, maybe a year, maybe longer… But, where we were, what we were doing, that is where we wanted to be, that is how we wanted to feel. We hoped it would last but then it was over. Maybe we tried to get back to that place but for whatever life reason we could not. Then, what are we left with? Only the memory and the desire to return.

Sure, this is where the poetry comes from. …This sense of living, remembering, and then longing. This is the birthplace for other art forms, as well. But, it is essential to note as you encounter each life experience is that it is here but it may never be here again. If you love it, love it totally as you may never feel it again.

It's Called Art
19/May/2017 07:26 AM

Most people do not follow a path of creating art. There are an untold number of reasons for this, as each of us were artists when we were children, but as adulthood comes on most people shift away from the practice of artistic creation. Though one could see this as an expected and accepted reality of life, a person moving away from the arts leaves the world with less. On the other hand, as so many people leave any artistic tendencies behind in their youth, this movement does clarify those who see art as a defining factor for their existence. Do you?

The fact is, the world does not support art. Yes, there are museums pretty much everywhere, but how many people actually go to them? Most people simply see going to a museum as a fieldtrip when they were in school or a necessity when they are on vacation. Most people do not go simply to go.

Once inside a museum, for most, instead of becoming a space of art appreciation, the museum becomes a space of judgment. For the abstract art, *"Anybody can do that!"* For the traditional art, *"I like that kind of stuff."*

But, art is much more than simply painting. It spans all gambits of reality. Yes, there are paintings and sculptures but there is also all the everything-else: from music, to photography, to poetry, to movies, the tea ceremony, the martial arts, even mowing the lawn and trimming plants can be an art form, onto how a person dresses. Art becomes art the moment a person consciously embraces what/anything they do as a form of art.

There are also the people who want to make a living from art. Are those people true artists? Or, are they simply businesspeople who have seen what a select few of others have done with a specific craft and follow in that path to gain fame and fortune? But, the fact is, though there are a certain percentage of people who enter into this pathway but a very-very-very few ever make a livelihood out of art, as it is nearly impossible.

Some people mimic art. They see what someone else has done and then try to reenact it. This is a very common practice—a practice that has been practiced throughout the centuries. But, is that true art or is that simply artistic imitation?

Art is a core representation of what is inside a person. Art is a something that must get out of a person. Whether that inside something is painting a painting, writing a word, playing a note, making a movie, or precisely dressing in a particular style. But, this practice is practiced by very few. Very few have the focused dedication to allow their life to be defined by art.

As stated, in childhood, we were all artists. When did you lose your art? Or, did you? Do you live a life of art? Or, are you simply one of those people when they see the artistic manifestations, created by others, that you simply gawk and judge?

The creation of art is the highest level of human expression. Can you leave behind what you have become and re-embrace the art and the artist inside of you that you knew as a child?

* * *
18/May/2017 01:52 PM

If you were told you were going to die tomorrow what would you do today?

* * *

18/May/2017 01:52 PM

Does what defined you then still define you now?

* * *
18/May/2017 07:14 AM

Do you own who and what you truly are or do you hide it from the world with lies, excuses, and justifications?

The Things You Do To Waste Your Time
18/May/2017 07:03 AM

In life, what are you doing right now? What are you doing that will get you to where you want to be?

Most people spend most of their life time screwing around. They find all kinds of reasons to not focus and pursue what they actually want to achieve in their life. This is why so many people are dissatisfied and unhappy with their life. …They do not focus and pursue their dreams.

People talk. People find emotional relationships to distract them. People make excuses about why they are doing what they are doing. People get drunk. But, very few take the time to focus their attention to the degree that they can actually achieve what they hope to achieve.

When I was a young instructor of the martial arts, many years ago, I would watch this pattern of behavior unfold time-after-time. People would come to my studio. Some came just for the health benefits of the martial arts, while others came to learn self-defense. That was great. They got what they paid for. Many, however, came with the hopes of earning their black belt. But, that takes time. That takes focus. That takes discipline. That takes dedication. And, very few people choose to possess any of those qualities because that takes mental determination. And, mental determination is one of the hardest qualities to develop within one's self. Thus, I watched as some did earn their black belts but most found an excuse to fall away from training.

It is the same with the film industry. I have watched this pattern forever. People want to be a star. Now, first of all, that is impossible. But, you can be an actor, you can be a filmmaker. This is especially the case in this digital age. You simple have to learn the craft and then do the craft. But, everyone wants everything handed to them. They do not want to work to achieve their dreams. They want it to be given to them. Thus, they pursue it for a time and then they walk away.

This mindset covers all aspects of life. People want, but they do not want to work for the achievement of what they want. This is why things like bars and the internet have destroyed the, *"What could have been,"* in so many people's lives. People find a distraction to waste their time and, thus, they do not do.

This is a life curse and it has been going on forever. But, it is you who has to decide what it is you truly want. It is you who has to decide if you are going to work and work and work until you achieve.

Excuses are easy. Distractions are easy to find. But, are you willing to focus your mind and move beyond those things and achieve what it is you actually want to achieve?

That's a question that can only be answered by you. Are you willing to focus, work, and not stop until you achieve?

*   *   *

17/May/2017 01:14 PM

Why does someone critique the life of another person? Because their own life is unfulfilled.

* * *
17/May/2017 01:10 PM

When someone has the propensity to speak negatively about others and about subjects that do not directly affect them it is very difficult to get that person to ever embrace a positive point of view.

The Personality of Philosophy
17/May/2017 07:25 AM

I came upon an interview that this one friend of my longtime Zen Filmmaking partner Donald G. Jackson had recently given where he discusses Don. I found it really sad that this guy actually knew Don longer than I did but he simply categorized him as incompetent filmmaker. He totally missed the point...

Now certainly, Don was a psychologically complicated narcissist who, due to his behavior, made a lot of enemies. But, he was far from an incompetent filmmaker. He was a philosophy-based filmmaker. And, that is the point I think many people miss about the man—I know this misunderstanding has occurred to me, as well.

I have spoken about this a lot over the year, but most people view all movies from a place of judgment. Very few people watch simply to see the art. They watch movies with a preconceived notion of what is to come next. They judge and compare any movie that they are currently watching with all of those they have seen before—particularly those with a very high budget where nothing more than the philosophy of making money was employed. But, a true aficionado of film does not frame their basis for judgment on dollars and cents. In fact, they don't judge at all. They simply watch and witness. The fact is, if you want to truly appreciate art, (whatever that art form may be), you need to see any creation for what it is, based upon its own reality of creation, and moreover, on the philosophy that it took to create it.

And... This is where the guy discussing Don completely missed the point. Don made his films based upon a philosophy of actualization. You may like or you may not like this philosophy, and what he created due to it, that is your choice. But, if you do not understand this as the entire basis for the films that Don created than you completely miss the point about the man as a filmmaker. Then, all you become is judge and jury. And, no one should judge art, that is just the wrong way to approach it.

I think this is a very important fact to think about as you pass through life, whenever you find yourself casting judgment. Who are you judging and why? What is the basis for your judgment? Do you know the facts about the person that you are judging? Do you actually understand the motivation for them creating art in the first place? And mostly, do you even comprehend the philosophy they were operating within when they were doing what they were doing—that thing you are casting judgment upon?

People who judge generally do not know, understand, or care about the facts of a person's philosophy. If they did, then there would be no judgment at all.

That's my judgment about judgment. ☺

* * *
16/May/2017 07:46 AM

The farther away you get from the noise the less you hear it.

No Need to Look for a Teacher
15/May/2017 01:20 PM

There are a lot of people out there who seek spiritual or life guidance. They look for a teacher to tell them what they should or should not do. But, there is truly no reason for this. You don't need a teacher. All you need to do is to open your eyes and witness the way people interact with life. From this, you will find all of the guidance that you need and you will know how you should or should not behave.

This morning I was driving through a parking lot en route to the post office. This guy came barreling into the parking lot. He was driving one of those new bright red Camaros. The kind of car that make anyone who is driving it look stupid. Anyway… As he raced in he was way over on my side of the road. So much so that I had to slam on my breaks and pull away from him. I threw my hands in the air. He drives up next to me and rolls down his window…

Now, here's the thing… I guess it may be because I live in a big city—the too many rats in cage syndrome. But, there are so many people that act so aggressively that it just ruins everything for everyone. Maybe they had a few months of Brazilian Jujitsu or MMA training so they think they can fight and they are always trying to break hard and intimidate people. But, I am not a person who is easily intimidated.

With his window rolled down, he scowls at me and says, *"This is a two lane road!"* Like what occurred was somehow my fault. I roll down my window and immediately respond, *"Yeah, but you're the one over the line,"* as I point to how his tires are way on my side of the road. Seeing that I was right, he drove off.

There you see the wrong way to behave.

A little bit later I was sitting outside at one of my frequent breakfast haunts enjoying my breakfast. (I always sit outside whenever I can). As the outdoor seating for this restaurant is right next to the parking lot this guy gets out of his car and hits his alarm which due to the enclosed nature of the patio I was sitting on loudly reverberated in the air. I turn around and looked at him.

First of all, why do people even set their car alarms? Nobody is going to break into your car. Nobody is going to steal your car. All that it does by hitting your alarm button and sounding your horn is disturb everyone in the vicinity.

Anyway, as he walked by me he said, *"Sorry, I didn't mean to do that."* Though the loudness still hurt my ears, at least he had the kindness in his heart to apologize for the mistake he made.

There you see the right way to behave.

Life is very easy if you make it easy. Knowing what to do and what not to do is very easy if you simply open your eyes and study the way other people behave thus guiding you to knowing how you would like to be treaded as opposed to how you would not like to be treated.

Be nice. Say good things. Do good things. Be forgiving. If you make a mistake don't try to cover it up with lies or aggression, just say you're sorry.

Someone to Love Someone to Hate
15/May/2017 08:10 AM

When each of us are young we find someone to love. …Someone out there. Someone we do not know. Maybe it is a music star, a movie star, a TV character, or a sport's personality. We choose that person to love by an untold plethora of abstract reasonings but, for whatever reason, we find them to be all that is appealing. We love them but we will never know them.

When we are young, some of us, also find someone to hate. These, *"Hates,"* are usually orchestrated by parents, family, or in some cases, friends. We are told someone is bad and, thus, as we are young and our discriminating minds are not fully developed, we believe what we are told and we hate them or that too.

As we pass through life, most people shift away from the abstract world of idol worship—of loving or hating with no actual basis for the emotion. They may like a person for what they do or the way they do it but they come to understand the difference between abstract/projected feelings and true feelings that are based upon actual interpersonal/physical relationships. They focus on what is <u>real</u> in their own life and shift their mind's concentration away from that abstract, unfounded world, of projected love and hate.

Though this is the case for most, it is not the case for everyone. This has particularly become the situation with the world of the internet, where so many people are removed from the actuality of true, personal relationships while replacing them with something that is not true, whole, or personal—only a perceived, projected reality that it only believed to be true. Simply look at a television show like MTV's Catfish to see all the beliefs that people hold while they are being totally deceived via the internet or social media.

In this world, what you can touch, you can know is real, everything else is abstract mental projections guided by what you want to believe or what you are told to believe.

Think about this, how much of what and/or who you love or you hate do you actually know anything about? Have you met the person you love or you hate? Have you practiced the craft of what you love or you hate? If you do not know the person, you cannot love or hate them as you have no actual and/or truthful basis for your emotion. If you have not mastered the craft that you love or you hate you have no actual accomplished basis for your emotion. Thus, if you follow this path, you are living your life based upon a lie of emotion(s). You may feel the emotion of love or of hate but it is not a true emotion as it is only based in your own mind that does not hold a true definition to actually draw a rational conclusion.

How do you live your life? Do you love or hate based upon speculation? If you do, you are wasting your life time as all you are doing is reinforcing the grasp that illusion has on this world.

Love is great. Do it. Hate is bad. Don't do it. But, whomever you love or you hate at least have the mental maturity to love or to hate them for the right reasons.

* * *
15/May/2017 07:09 AM

If…

Seeking Forgiveness
13/May/2017 07:54 AM

In this blog and in my talks and other writings I often discuss the interplay of human interaction. I do this because most people never even think about this subject. They go through life doing whatever it is they want to do and they care not about the consequences. They care not unless something negative happens to them. Then, at that point, it is all that they think about.

I believe that the people who read this blog are not like that, however. But, people who actually consciously consider the impact they are having on this Life Space and on the lives of other people are few and far between. They are on the peripheries of human society. Most people are driven by very self-serving motivations. And, that is sad. A lot of lives and Life Times are damaged by this style of behavior.

As we pass through life, each of us is going to do something that hurts someone else. But, it is what we do after that point that defines us as human beings.

Think about this, have you hurt someone? Did you inflict that injury with conscious intent? If you did, that makes you a very bad person. If you justified your actions in your own mind and/or to other people that makes you a worse person.

On the other hand, have you, like most of us have, hurt someone but did not set out to do so? Once you realized that you have hurt someone, what were your actions? Did you care enough to set about on a course of action to correct what you had done or did you simply say, *"Sorry."*

Here lies the definition of who you truly are as a human being and what will be your overall impact on the life of others. Most of us, as we pass through life, do something that injures another person either physically or psychologically. Some people actually acknowledge what they have done and ask for forgiveness. But saying, *"Sorry,"* means nothing if you do not set out to right your wrong.

As stated, the majority of people in this world are very self-serving. They care not about others. They do not care about the damage they cause, nor do they seek forgiveness. Plus, many feel that they have the right to say or do anything they want as long as that action does not negatively affect their own life. It's sad, but that is how most people operate. But, it doesn't have to be like that. You can care, if you care enough to care. For what does injuring the life of another person truly equal? And, how does that injury make you or your life any better?

Many people, as they damage the life of another person, do so believing that they are right in doing so. Maybe they are judging a person which causes harm to that person's life or livelihood. Maybe they are treating a person unfairly; not taking who they truly are into consideration. Perhaps they are even physically injuring them. All of things, if they are consciously set about in their doing, have no great benefit to this overall Life Space. Judgment is never fact; it is only opinion. How you treat a person sets a whole, never-ending, course of events into motion and if you are the sourcepoint of those events it will be you who ultimate encounters the consequences. If you actually physically hurt someone, you may have won the battle but it will be you, due to your negative actions, who will ultimately lose the war in life.

At best, all a person who lives a life of judgment and unthinking behavior is doing is claiming I am right and you are wrong. But, who is ultimately to say? If you live your life from this space of external judgment, all you do is create damage; you help no one. As no one is helped, all that is happening is that people are injured. From this, no good is born in your life or the life of the world around you. Thus, as you are the sourcepoint of the negativity you will ultimately be the one who pays the price for unleashing it.

This brings us back to the point of, do you actually care about the actions that you are unleashing. Can you step outside of yourself long enough to realize that you have done something wrong, ask for forgiveness from the person or persons you have injured, and then set about on a course of repairing what you have broken? As most people are ego driven, this rarely happens. This is why the world is in the condition it is in. People only care about themselves but they don't care about you and they don't about me.

Ask yourself, how do you interact with life? Do you cause damage with your thoughts, words, or actions? If and when you do, are you Man-Enough (or Woman-Enough) to own your actions, actually understand that what you have done is wrong and has hurt somebody and then set about on a course to erase what you have done? If you are, that is great! You make the world a better place! If you are not, that is bad! You make the world a worse place! And, as you have hurt someone, you too will be hurt. That is just the law of the universe…

Any damage that you have created and not repaired not only damages the life of the person your inflicted the damage upon but it defines you as a person as you were not conscious and/or caring enough to set about on a course of repairing that damage.

What do you believe becomes of a person who hurts other people? Don't justify your reasons. Don't make excuses. Don't try to turn the blame around on someone else. Just answer the question.

*   *   *
12/May/2017 04:53 PM

If you are claiming that you are helping someone while you hurt someone else in the process, your premise is completely flawed.

You Can See Your Destiny in the Lives of Other People
12/May/2017 08:18 AM

Throughout life we pass through a very limited timeframe doing what we do. This doing is based upon what available options are available to us. The options we choose—the actions we choose to make are based upon personal choice. You decide to do something because you believe it is the right thing for you to do. You decide what is the right thing for you to do based upon what you desire and what you see other people have received by doing what they have done.

But, life is more than simply you wanting to be someone or having something. Life is about the experience you have while passing from birth to death. Your life is defined by how you behave at each moment of your life—the things that you do during the experience of each experience. That is what comes to define you as a person and the life contributions you will or will not make.

Most people look outside of themselves as they decide what to desire. They want to be a *"This,"* or a *"That."* That want to possess, *"That."* They want it because they believe that by achieving something or by owning something it will bring them happiness and fulfillment. Maybe… But, that is one of the ultimate paradoxes of life. What one person feels when they reach a specific plateau is not what another person will experience. Even though the achievement may be the same, the personal experience will be very different.

Do you ever study people? Do you ever watch the way specific people behave in specific circumstances? Do you ever witness the way people act and react to situations? Do you ever watch a particular person, who is doing what you want to do, who possesses what you want to own, as they pass through their life?

Taking the time to consciously witness another person's life experience and life action(s) is one of the most revealing ways to not only understand the commonality of the life experience but to study what will come next as you pass towards achieving your desires.

Have you ever met a person who is doing what you hope to do? Have you ever walked down the road of achieving what you want to achieve and then you realize that you are behaving in a very similar manner to the person you once witnessed walking ahead of you on the same path to achievement that you are on?

Most people never take the time to do this. They never take the time to study people. They are generally so locked within their own heads that they either do not care or they do not have the mental potential to look beyond themselves. They may make judgments about people but they never take the time to truly study a person. This style of behavior is due to one of the primary conditions of human existence that many people suffer from; selfishness.

The problem with operating from this mindset is, however, that most people never take the time to actually see what is coming next. If they did, many life obstacles would and could be avoided. But, they don't look so they don't see.

Seeing yourself in other people is easy. It happens to all of us. Many people make the comment, *"Oh, I've become my mother or my father."* As you are rudimentarily founded in the behavior that your parent's exhibited this is an obvious example. But, as you go through life, you also become influenced by other people that you spend time with. As most people do not study this style of symbiotic relationship they never consciously witness the influences of other people taking hold on their life. Thus, if they associate with less than compassionate, caring, mentally aware, and giving people, (as most of us are forced to do as we pass through life), they enter onto the road of embracing negativity and leaving a negative footprint on life.

The answer to this quandary is simple, *"Look before you leap."* Take the time to open your mind's eye and actually study the people you interact with. As you walk the road to your desired achievement, though you may not have the absolute choice as to whom you do or do not associate with, you will at least be able to see what is coming next if you behave and interact with life in a prescribed, specific manner. By watching and witnessing others you can see what may be to come in your life. From this, you can make the conscious choice of what you ultimately want to do and who you ultimately want to become.

*   *   *
11/May/2017 09:45 AM

When you decide to interact with someone are you thinking about them or are you thinking about you?

* * *
11/May/2017 09:38 AM

If someone has come into your life and damaged your life they are probably not going to be conscious enough to care about the problems they have created so it is better to look elsewhere for help than to waste your time expecting that person to care enough to care.

What Are You Going to Do When?
11/May/2017 08:34 AM

Throughout a person's life, people do things that come to define who they are. What you do today has the potential to define what you will be tomorrow.

Young people, as they are passing through to adulthood, forever seem to be the most apt at doing something that will come to define their later years. Though they are the most vulnerable to making bad choices, adults also make choices that either negatively or positively affects their life everyday. Whether it is smoking, drinking, taking drugs, stealing, getting arrested, having unprotected sex, charging things on your credit card, getting a tattoo, leaning how to play a musical instrument, studying the martial arts or dance, being a studious student who tries very hard in school, or an employee who either slacks off or excels at their job, each of these things can and will define the rest of a person's life. And, for the most part, each of these events is entered into by choice.

Obviously, doing something knowingly positive is an individual's conscious attempt at making their tomorrow a better place. But, this is commonly not the case. Throughout a person's life they do things that will define their tomorrow but they do it with little thought as to the long term ramifications of what they are doing.

In our current, modern, western culture, getting massive amounts of tattoos has become the norm. In times gone past, this was a limited practice. Now, everywhere you look, people have tattoos up and down their body, on their neck, on their face, you name it.

This is obviously a very physical example of this subject. But, what about tomorrow? What about when you no longer want the tattoo? Yes, via painful, expensive, laser treatments some tattoos can be removed—some but not all. But, what if you've had them done, you no longer want them, perhaps they are hampering your life advancement, but you don't have the money to get them removed? Then what?

The future life of a person is also defined by whom they associate with. The people one lets into their life comes to define their life.

Who you know and what you do with whom you know sets the stage for your tomorrow. In some cases, the people you choose to associate with have the potential to make your tomorrow a vastly better place. In other cases, it is just the opposite.

This also goes to the definitive fact(s) of interpersonal psychology. Are you a good person to be friends with? Is your life defined by long standing friendships that lead to positive life experiences or has your life been defined by chaotic interpersonal relationships? As you are the sourcepoint for all you choose to encounter, how are you and your personal psychological makeup responsible for your interpersonal encounters?

Many people over look this fact as they pass through life. Though they may have encountered one turbulent relationship after the next, they never look to themselves as the source for this problem as it is always easier to blame someone else.

What you choose to do at each stage of your life—where you choose to put yourself at each stage of your life—who you choose to associate with at each stage of your life—how you choose to behave within any relationship at each stage of your life sets up what you will encounter next in your life.

What are you doing today to define your tomorrow? Is what you are doing today going to orchestrate a negative or a positive tomorrow?

* * *
10/May/2017 06:03 PM

Just because you deny doing something does not mean that you didn't do it.

No Personal Interpretations
10/May/2017 07:50 AM

I have a friend who is currently in grad school. They had written a final paper for a class and when they received it back from the instructor the professor had provided the expected critique; as all instructors do. In brief, what the professor said was that at this level there is no room for personal interpretations or judgments. All words should be based upon factual references with no personal perceptions. Meaning, do not elaborate and add your own thoughts, as my friend had done, just present the facts.

I found this to be very interesting and a shift in what I had come to learn. Having spent a good amount of time in grad school myself, I too wrote tons and tons of papers. But, at least in my field of study, interpretation is kind of what you did. You would research and write a paper on a particular subject and then provide an analysis. Many times, that analysis would be based upon your interpretation of what you had learned.

Now, this was not always the case. I think back to one paper I wrote for a class. It was on this one author who came to fame in the 1960s. His style of writing was to take what he had learned from various Eastern schools of thought and then present a mishmash of the knowledge within the page of his books. I always found this style of writing a bit disingenuous and I said so in my paper. The instructor returned my paper, not liking what I had written. In essence, stating the same thing as the aforementioned professor had said. Thus, I had to rewrite the entire paper. What I surprisingly found in doing so, however, was I came to a new appreciation for the author.

That's what school is, a process of learning. You are told to do something in a particular manner, and then, you must do it even if you don't want to. I think this mindset is something that is missing from the lives of many people;

they have no sense of refined (forced if you will) mental discipline. They just say and do what they want and from this life damage and chaos is born.

I remember back to when I was an undergrad and I had a professor who said something very profound. He stated, it didn't matter what major you focused your studies upon but studying at a university teaches you how to think. I believe that is vey true. Especially at the graduate level.

Anyway, I believe this is an important thing to look at as you pass through life. How much of what you do is based upon what you think but not based upon facts, simply personal impressions? Now, I imagine some would argue that this is the way life is supposed to be experienced, upon feelings. But, feelings are often times false interpretations of reality and are deceptive. Feelings are based upon emotion, and emotions change.

I think back to a personal incident I had happen to me a number of years ago—relating to this subject. I have written about it before… Anyway, I was dumbstruck when this university employed Ph.D. wrote this whole discourse about my life and me and placed it on one of the martial arts newsgroups. He even used a footnote style of referencing to make it look official. He grabbed stuff from my website and other places and used the piece to bash me. Personally, I thought it was so funny but that's just who I am. *"So, National Enquirer,"* as I called it then. For those of you who may not know, *The National Enquirer* was (and I guess still is) one of those celebrity rags that were sold at the cashier counter of supermarkets and it probably currently has an online presence, as well. But, this guy's piece was based solely upon perceived interpretations of my life and it was harshly slanted. It was done in a manner to damage my life. And, I suppose to the mind of those who do not have the perception to see through this style of attack, it did. I always wondered why a university employed Ph.D. would do that? Anyway…

But, here we get to the whole purpose of this piece. There is something truly good about what that professor said in their critique. They stated that writing should be based solely upon established facts—not perceived facts, not desired facts, not limited facts, not personally motivated interpretations of the facts, but fact whole and true onto themselves. I don't know... Doesn't that seem like a better way to live your life and to make your decisions?

*   *   *
10/May/2017 07:48 AM

Most of the things you do in life you do them simply because you think that you are suppose to do them.

* * *
10/May/2017 07:48 AM

Casting judgments is easy. Making yourself a better person is hard.

How Do People Describe You?
09/May/2017 07:19 AM

Most people are only concerned with what they think about other people. They never think about what other people are thinking about them.

Do you ever ponder how people describe you? Now, I am not talking about someone who has never met you. Those people do not know what they are talking about and should never be brought into the conversation. I am speaking about someone who actually knows you. What do they think about you? How do they describe you?

We each pass through life interacting with an untold number of people. Whatever that number is, that total is big. Most people we see, we pass, but we never personally interact with. Others we have brief interactions with. Though those people may have an impression of us, but as they have not spent any real time getting to know us, they cannot truly have formed a valid opinion. But then, there are those people who have known us for an extended period of time, those are the people who at least seemingly know who and what we are. How do those people describe you?

In each interpersonal interaction we have as we pass through life, we encounter people in very specific manners for very specific reasons. When we are young, some people we meet while we are in school. As we get older, perhaps we work with people and we know them through our employment. There is, of course, family. But, those relationships are more or less forced upon us. We interact with those people not so much by choice but by necessity. Then, there are those people we choose to associate with. We can call them friends. Whether these relationships go on for a short period of time or for years, those are the people that arguably know us the best as we are the most natural in those situations. How do the people that make up these various groups describe you?

As we pass through life, and have our interpersonal interactions, each of the people we interact with comes to form an opinion about us. It is important to note that many of these opinions are based upon personal projections. Meaning, many people never see a person as they truly are, all they see is what they want to see. This style of interpersonal definition is most commonly based upon having a certain hope or a desire that will occur by being in whatever type of relationship with a specific person. In other words, these are relationships based upon projected desires. Generally, these are the style of relationship that do not end well. A person wants something. And, they want what they want to occur in a specific fashion. If they get what they want out of the relationship, all is good. If they do not, all becomes bad. Thus, they will describe anyone based upon their fulfillment or the lack thereof of their personal desires. These are the type of personal descriptions to be wary of. Thus, if someone is speaking about a person that they claim they know, you should always question why that individual is saying what they are saying about the person of whom they speak, especially if what they are saying is based upon negativity.

Each of us evolves as we pass through life. We are born with a core personality and then we are indoctrinated into life via a series of personal experiences that only we experience. Many of us become better versions of our self as we get older. These are the conscious people. The people who seek to become better. There is also the other side of the coin. Those are the people who devolve as they pass through life. Those are the people who find their life unfilled, thus, they become angry, mean-spirited, or even violent. As you listen to any definition provided to you by an individual about another person, it is also very important to find out not only how but when this individual knew the person they are describing. People change as they pass through life. It is as simple as that. And, you really need to take that fact into consideration when you listen to any opinion being given to you about a specific person. When did that individual know the person they describe?

So, how do people describe you? Do you ever think about this fact? Do you care? Do you ever look back through your past and question how does a specific person feel about you? How are you being remembered by that person? How do they speak of you, if they ever mention you at all?

We each interact with an untold number of people as we pass through life. How many of the people that you have interacted with do you believe actually knew who you truly are? Do you hide who you really are from others? Do you lie about who and what you are to others? How are you remembered and why? You should take some time and think about this.

Random Acts of Violence
07/May/2017 08:48 AM

I was walking down the walkway to the Santa Monica Pier yesterday...

First of all, let me prefaces this by saying, I have not been there in years. As a kid and a teenager I loved the Santa Monica Pier. It was fun place to go. I took my first date, in 7th grade, to the beach and the pier where she spent all my money at the penny arcade. ...All the money I was saving-up to buy an electric guitar. Lesson learned... ☺

As an adult, I shot a movie there and as an actor I did a role in a TV show on the pier. But, for some reason, they didn't give me screen credit when the show was broadcast. That always bothered me. But, that's Hollywood, they do what they want! ☺

Anyway, as the years have gone by, the place has just become a major tourist attraction. Plus, it has also become overrun with the homeless and the crazies. So many people! It's a mess! The last time I was there was maybe ten years ago. I went there to see Patti Smith when she was relaunching her touring career and she was doing a concert. But, I only stayed for a few songs. She and her band were still great but it ain't the seventies anymore... That's the backstory...

Anyway, my lady and I were shopping in the nearby Promenade and she suggested that we walk down to the pier. Sure, why not... It was a very cool and windy May day. That's great! I love it. We walked over and began our descent down the walkway. It was extremely crowded as many of the late afternoon crowds were leaving and many were still going to the pier. As it is a relatively small sidewalk, it was real *elbow-to-elbow* human traffic. We were stuffed in there.

We are about half way down the walkway and I see a young guy with long hair walking upward. All of sudden he puts out his shoulders, kind of like a football player does when they get ready to charge someone, and when he walks by me he forcefully smacks me in the shoulder with his shoulder but then keeps going. *"What a dick!"* I exclaim. But, he's gone.

Why he did this is anybody's guess. Why a person would behave like that, who knows? And, if he did it to me, I'm sure he will do it to someone else. …Someone else who may not be so forgiving. But, this all details the abstract way some people encounter life. It also goes to the negative way some people interact with others in life. I am sure, in his mind, he had a sense of logic for why he wanted to give me a shoulder impact. Maybe he hates crowds. Maybe he hates blondes. Maybe he hates guys who wear sport coast and fedoras. Maybe he hates interracial couples. Maybe he hates me. Maybe it was just random. I will never know. And, in fact, I really don't care. But, if you think about it, this is how so many people behave in life. They puff up, they hit, then they hide in the crowd. They try to do damage, for whatever misplaced logic, but that damaged serves no greater purpose. They just want to lash out.

In fact, just this week in Las Vegas, some guy decided to sucker punch a father in the back of the head for no reason and the man actually died. And, this is the type of unexpected occurrence that may occur from this style of behavior. As there are cameras everywhere in Vegas they got the guy who did this. But, the man is still dead. He was murdered. What did this violence prove? Why are random acts of unfocused physical violence seemingly on the rise?

From a psychological perspective we can understand that people who behave in this manner have some misdirected anger—anger that they have never come to terms with. In fact, people who behave in this fashion may be mentally ill. But, this style of person is everywhere around us. They exist in all of the crowds and all of the masses. Are you one? Are you a person who does damage due to your misplaced psychological anger? …Because a person that is content in life, whole and complete within themselves, has no need to be offensive towards anyone for any reason.

You see, we all like what we like, just as we all dislike what we dislike. That's just life. But, most of us understand our feelings are just our feelings and we know that it is right to control them—we don't unleash negativity to the world. We don't say bad things; we don't do bad things. If we bump into someone we say, *"Sorry."*

But, some people aren't like that. Due to their anger at life, at their life-situation, at themselves, they lash out. And, from this, comes damage. Damage to the lives of other people. And, that's just not right. There is no rational logic nor is there is any self-defined logic for that style of behavior. It is simply wrong.

So, what does all this mean? It means that every now and then we all are going to encounter this style of a person as we pass through life. We will be in a crowd of a million people, all of them living their life, doing what they are doing to the best of their ability, hurting no one, and some jerk is going to be in the crowd deciding to bump you shoulder-to-shoulder and then hide in the masses. They are a sad person but they are out there hiding in the deluge.

But, it has to be understood, people who behave in this fashion, nothing positive ever comes of their life. For that guy, this will be the only place in history that he will ever be mentioned.

If you want to live a good life and make a truly positive contribution, the only way to do that is to do positive things. Never let yourself justify yourself into performing negative actions. Good is good, it is as simply as that. Good never hurts anyone no matter what the justification.

* * *
07/May/2017 08:01 AM

What do people see when they look at you?

The Craziness of the Airlines
05/May/2017 08:25 AM

With all of the craziness of and on airlines that is currently taking place... ...I mean, old doctors are getting forcefully dragged off of planes, men are kicked off of their flight because they really had to use the bathroom really-bad at a time the stewardess deemed inappropriate, plane stewards are getting accosted by passengers after they mess with a crying female passenger and her baby, a crazed guy starting an onboard fight with another passenger, and families are thrown off a flight after not wanted to give up a seat for their baby that they paid for. I mean come on... But, do you think that this stuff hasn't been going on forever? Thankfully, we have entered into an age where everything is taped on our phones so there is proof. But, as someone who has spent a lot of time in the sky, I can tell you all kinds of craziness goes on all the time.

Now, first of all, I must say, my experiences in the sky have never been too bad. I mean, there have been a few scary times but that was more due to the weather. I remember as a young child flying with my mother, we were in the middle of a very-very bad storm before planes could climb above them, and the plane was bouncing all over the place—like in those movies. One time, flying out of Hong Kong, the pilot thought it was great idea to takeoff, literally, in the eye of a hurricane (typhoon). Wrong... I was on a plane that had some serious problems so that had to emergency land in Sapporo. Flying to Hawaii one time the plane started leaking fuel so they had to dump the remaining fuel over the ocean, return to LAX, and land with a full array of fire trucks and ambulances surround the runway. But, I emerged safe and sound.

Mostly, it is the people that cause the problems. I've had a few uncomfortable experiences. One of them came when I was flying out of Karachi and the South Asian man siting next was coughing and coughing and coughing. I mean, the whole flight to Paris. It was bad. It was not a cold it was probably TB. But, what could I do? Though I did get tested when I got back to the States. It was scary. Another time, flying out of Colombo, the South Asian guy next to me slipped off his plastic slippers, pulled down his food tray, and put his dirty feet up on it. Not good! But again, what could I do?

On the more physical side, one time flying to Delhi, a drunkenly crazed South Asian passenger went nuts. His friend and the stewardess try to come him down but then he started to fight. Did I think to join in and take him down? Sure. But, in those situations, it is always better to let it play out and wait until it gets serious and they really need help before jumping in. They finally got him under control.

And, that's the thing... If you are nice, things generally remain nice. I mean there was a time flying out of Tokyo that they had overbooked the flight. I go to check in and I found that they kicked me out of my first class seat and stuck me in the back of the plane in economy. I was pissed! I had paid a lot of money for that ticket. And now, I was stuck with all of the people who a paid a fraction of what I had paid, getting far less service. Was I mad? Sure. Did I start a big commotion? No. The desk person promised me I would get a refund when I returned. Did I ever get one? No. I contacted the airline but, *"Sorry..."* Now, that's messed up but my throwing a fit would have changed nothing.

A few years ago, (maybe ten or more now), there used to be a reality television show on the air called, *"Airline,"* where they showed all the interworking of Southwest Airlines. You witnessed as a lot of people got fucked over by the airline and got very mad. But, some were cool. They just rolled with the punches. And, that is my advice. You have to be nice. You have to be cool. Sure, you may not like what is taking place. You can calmly voice your opposition but they, the airlines, hold all the cards. So, you cannot win.

With all of the recent goings-on, and the airlines being called in front of Congress and all that, there have been some changed promised. But, those are by U.S. based airlines. What about all the rest?

The thing is, we are all people interacting on an interactive level in an interactive life. Thus, we have to interact. Most people are nice—or they at least try to be. Others are combative and rude. That's just life! Who are you? If you want to find fights, you can find them. But, all that does to your life is place you in a never ending realm of confrontation. This is never good. This is never what a conscious person does.

So, when the shit goes down on an airline or elsewhere, just be calm—just be nice. Then, you will pass from here to there in your life with more joy and less blood. And, the fact is, at the end of the day, a fight is never worth fighting.

Set the Example
05/May/2017 07:11 AM

Next time you encounter someone saying something negative about something or someone or being unkind, disrespectful, or inconsiderate in their words or their actions stop them/correct them—let them know that is the wrong way to behave and inform them that someone cares about interacting in only a positive manner.

* * *
04/May/2017 09:04 AM

If you're not saying something nice, you're saying something that shouldn't be said.

*   *   *
04/May/2017 08:30 AM

When something negative happens to a person they never look to themselves and their previous actions as a possible cause, they simply try to blame someone else.

This is why the field of karma is forever replenishing.

* * *

04/May/2017 07:40 AM

Used to be… What does that even mean?

Who Are You Trying to Impress?
AKA You Did It, Now What?
04/May/2017 07:32 AM

In each of our lives we choose what we are going to do—we decide what we are going to do next. I always emphasize that this is a situation that uniquely happens in the Free World. For if you are out there living in one of the war torn regions of the world or if you are starving in a country that is devastated by famine you have no choice to do anything but try to survive. That is why I find it very troubling that so many people, here in the Free World, waste so much of their time Doing and Pursuing things that lead to no greater good and/or no world betterment.

What do you do? Why do you do it? Who are you trying to impress by Doing what you are Doing? What do you think what you are Doing will prove? And, you did what you did, now what?

I was reading someone post on Facebook the other day. The person was asking people not to be too harsh about what they created. Someone commented, *"That's what the internet is. People are mean on the internet."* And this, in some cases, is very true.

That comment goes to the entire question that you need to ask yourself as you are Doing what you are Doing. The fact is, so many people waste so much of their Doing living in a world of negativity or inactivity simply by perusing the internet. That, in and of itself, is not a bad thing but it is a, *"Thing."* And, as such, being a, *"Thing,"* it comes to define a person's life.

Anything you do comes to define your life. Again, we go back to the question, *"Why are you doing what you are doing and who are you trying to impress?"*

Most people live in a very mindless space. They do what they do without consciously thinking about anything they are Doing. They do what they do so they will be liked, so they will find friends, and so that they will be accepted. But, here again we go to the perils of life lived in the Free World; i.e. people waste their time and do only things that mean nothing. They do what they do defined by where they find themselves. And, if they live their life on the internet, believing that any of it is real, they will, someday, wake up and see their entire life was lived in the abstract world of anti-reality and untruth(s).

Some people have a very focused mindset and they set out to accomplish something. Most people are not like that, however. They simply are lead along through life, guided by family, friends, culture, religion, and desire. These are the people that end up at the culmination of their life with nothing to show for it. This is not good or bad, this is simply the way that it is.

Yet, in Doing Nothing, these people are Doing Something. Though they are not Doing a Conscious Nothing, like in Zen, but due to the unconsciousness of their activity, they add to the greater clogging of this Life Space. As they do nothing, nothing better is unleashed.

On the other hand, there are the people who are driven and they, *"Do."* But, how many Doers that you know are Doing something for the betterment of all. They may be lying to themselves and to you by believing what they are Doing is helping someone. But, if one person is at the source of the Doing and one person receives the rewards for the Doing, this Doing is only ego-based Doing. From this, nothing good is ever born.

Again, who are you? Why do you do what you do? Do you ever ask yourself this question?

It is time to ponder that question. Once you have the answer to that question, ask yourself, *"What has what you have done, done to others?"* And, *"Was what you have done a help or was it a hurt?"* It what you have done has hurt anyone, what you have done is bad and can only be judged as such.

Most people never take the time to look at themselves, question what they are Doing, find out the reason why, and view what their Doing has done to others. Is this how you operate in your life? If you do, you really need to look at yourself as if you are hurting instead of helping, if you are achieving instead of relieving, all your life will equal is further damage to a world that is already in excruciating pain.

Care about other before you care about yourself.

Have You Ever Met a Normal Person Who Claimed to Be a Psychic, a Clairvoyant, a Channel, or a Guru?
03/May/2017 09:05 AM

Most people never delve into the realm of metaphysics. Sure, they hear about it on TV or in the movies—they may hear stories about the great things that this person has predicated or they may even see commercials about psychics while watching their favorite TV show. But, most people never look any deeper. And, this is a good thing.

Have you ever, personally, met a person who claimed to be a psychic, a clairvoyant, a guru, or anything like that? Probably not. You have never sought them out so finding them was not necessary. But, if you have ever interacted with one of these people or have gotten to know that person on any interpersonal level, then you will witness their flaws.

Think about this, why does any-one claim to be any-thing of metaphysical rank? There is no school they went to and received a degree in the subject. There is no State Board that they must prove their qualifications to and then pass a test. Nope... They just claim to be what they claim to be and the world look out.

Though I had been in close contact with a number of people who were known to be a, *"Guru,"* throughout my teen years, it was not until I first arrived in India that I encountered a so-called, *"Psychic."*

I had arrived in Deli the night before. My plane landed at about 2:00 AM. I got a taxi and made my way to my hotel but I was so jetlagged that I did not sleep. When the sun rose I hit the streets. Young, I did not sense the danger that is everywhere in India. I just walked through the dirty streets... I first randomly ended up at a Mosque and then at a temple. Finally, I made my way to Connaugth Place, which was then the central shopping area in New Deli. There, I was accosted by a, *"Psychic."* He claimed he could tell me all kinds of things and from this I would gain the blessings of the gods. Oh, and by the way, the guy had leprosy. Anyway, I knew it was bullshit, but I played along. He told me I was in India to find enlightenment. I smiled... Okay, that was easy to figure out, look at my untrimmed long hair, my beard, and the way I was dressed in yogi attire. He went on for a while telling me all the expected nonsense. Then, he wanted payment for his services. And, he informed me, if I didn't pay him, my trip would be cursed. I laughed. But sure, whatever... I gave him some money. It worked out to only be a few dollars as the exchange rate was so high back then. ...He got to eat that night and I did learn some important lessons.

Here's the thing, so called, *"Psychics,"* are very adept in studying a person and gaining quick insight into them. I mean, look at any person you see on the street and you too can gain insight into their personality and the motivations for their life: how are they dressed, what is the style of their hair, are they a clean and well-put together person or are they sloppy, are their shoes polished, do they wear an expensive watch or jewelry, any religious symbolism, and so on... It is very easy to quickly understand the foundations of a person if you simply look. This is the first clue that psychics use to feed you information about yourself and make you believe they know something deep about you. Then, they ask you probing question. How you answer those questions gives them their next level of insight into who they determine you to be.

It's a con game... Anybody can do it. The thing is, most people don't want to do it. They don't want to make themselves look like something all-knowing and they don't want to take advantage of people. But, there are a lot of lost, uncaring, out of control people out there who all they care about is themselves and how they are viewed by the world. They want to be seen as something that someone else is not. They don't care who they hurt in the process of them claiming to be a metaphysical something. They are just doing what they are doing to do make themselves look like something more. And, the saddest part of this equation is that some of these people are so lost that they actually believe their own lie.

The best, most amusing thing to do, if you want to play games with a psychic is to not give them wholly truthful answers to their questions and watch them run away on a false tangent. Or, ask them a question that they have no way of knowing the answer to. Then, watch them make excuses…

Here's the other thing to be careful of, some psychics actually investigate their clients. For example, for someone like me, there's a lot of my biographical information out there. And, in this age of the internet, that is true for most people. So, never get hooked in if a psychic is basing what they are telling you on something that they could have found out some where else in cyberspace or by asking your acquaintances questions about you and so on.

Okay, now that they have been debunked, we can ask the question why does anyone claim anything. Mostly, they are the people who have not achieved anything with their life. Take a look at these people who claim the grandeur of metaphysical titles. What have the done prior to doing that? Like I always say, if you have not spent time formally living as a monk, you have never developed true inner discipline. Yes, you may have nurtured and developed your ego but you have no true understanding of the essence of spirituality. Thus, claiming metaphysical title is false and bogus.

But, more than that, who are these people? I cannot tell you how many times I have been forced to interact with the so-called, *"Metaphysical Something's,"* and they were the most false, ego driven, emotionally out of control people I have ever met. If you are not whole onto yourself, if you are not in control of your emotions, if you are not guided by the higher sense of self and are not dedicated to selfless service, then you have no business claiming any metaphysical title or aptitude.

So… Before you buy into anything anyone is selling, think about these things. A true holder of knowledge does not claim to be a holder of knowledge. A true teacher does not charge for their teachings.

* * *

02/May/2017 07:47 PM

If you've done something that damaged the life of another person, either through your words or your actions, and you've done nothing to repair the damage you've unleashed, that means whatever you've broken is still broken.

As another person is defined by the damage that you caused, how do you think that will effect the evolution of your life?

Good People Do Good Things
01/May/2017 07:32 AM

How much of your Life-Time do you spend angry? How much of your Life-Time do you spend dissatisfied? How much of your Life-Time do you spend wishing you were somebody else, doing something else? How much of your Life-Time do you spend blaming someone or something for your current circumstance? How much of your Life-Time do you spend criticizing other people? How much of your Life-Time do you spend doing things that negatively affect the Life-Time of other people? How much of your Life-Time do you spend taking things that aren't yours simply because you believe that you can? How much of your Life-Time do you spend justifying your actions? How much of your Life-Time do you spend actually trying to hurt other people? How much of your Life-Time do you spend not caring about who or what you hurt? If you spend any of your Life-Time doing any of these things you are not living a good life.

Living a good life is defined by doing good things. What are good things? Things that hurt no one but help many. What kind of person does these things? A good person.

What defines a good person? A good person is someone who consciously focuses their life to the degree that if they have or if they encounter less than ideal life issues they learn to master them instead of being mastered by them. They are in control of their mind to the degree that they do not allow negative emotions to control them. If they feel them, they take control over them. They address the cause, find a conscious pathway to correct them, and then move forward.

If you are not a good person, that means you are a bad person. What happens to bad people? What occurs to them is that due to the negative emotions they allow to control their life, they say and do negative things. From this is born a world of dissatisfaction, anger, pain, frustration, envy, and suffering that continually repeats itself due to the actions being unleashed by that person.

Your life can be a good and happy place. But, happiness begins by caring enough to care—not only about yourself and the one's you care about but about all of those you encounter in life and all of those you think about.

Your thoughts and your words create your actions. Your actions create your life and what you will next encounter. It is very simple, doing good things equals good things, doing bad things equals bad things.

Who do you want to be in life: bad or good? What do you want to spread in life: bad or good? How do you want to be remember in life: bad or good?

Encounter the bad with the good. Do this to your self and spread this to the world. Good is always better then bad. Never embrace the bad. Be good.

Everybody Wants Something from Me but Nobody Ever Gives Me Anything
30/Apr/2017 10:40 AM

I have long made the semi-joking statement, *"Everybody wants something from me but nobody ever gives me anything."* But, when it comes right down to the reality of it, that is how my life has played out.

Recently, there have been a lot of people asking me if they can distribute Donald G. Jackson's or my films. ...This, at the point in history when distribution is exceedingly easy, anyone can set up a company, and do print-on-demand. But, do these people ever ask themselves, *"Why would I want them to make money distributing my films?"* Like the joking statement I have made as an actor in several of my films, *"What's in it for me?"* ...I mean, I own a distribution company, why do I need you? It is not like these people offer me vast amount of money. Then, it may be a different story. But, they do not. They just want what they want for free. ...Do you have any idea the amount of time, energy, creativity, and money it takes to make a movie? And, you expected me to give all that to someone I do not even know?

Here's where we reach one of the philosophic quandaries of life; i.e., people want what they want for free. They want what someone else has. They want what someone else has achieved. They want it, but they do not want to work for it. When they see someone with it, they either want to steal it or, if they have some-what of a conscience, they ask if they can have it.

My answer is, *"No."*

Throughout my life I have always been more than happy to help people. I have always been happy to take people along for the ride. I came of age in a time and a space of doing karma yoga AKA selfless service—doing something and expecting nothing in return. But, that does not mean giving someone my livelihood or letting them make money off of something they had nothing to do with creating.

But, times have changed from the days of caring about the well-being of others and doing karma yoga… People see the vastness of life and cyberspace and how taking what someone else has done and/or flat out stealing it has become easy and, in fact, the norm. But, this is just wrong! If you achieve anything in life by doing this, you have developed exceedingly bad karma. And, then what comes next?

Donald G. Jackson was the last person I can actually put my finger on who went out of his way to help me in a focused manner. But, there was a very high price to pay for that relationship. Yet, I made him a promise to keep his filmmaking legacy alive and I have done my best to do so. So, I hope I have repaid his actions.

Most people are not like that, however. They don't want to help anyone unless there is something in it for them. They want to take; they do not want to make. …And this is where all of the problems of the world arise.

So, how do you encounter life? Are you the point of inception? Or, are you the one trying to make a name for yourself or a dollar off of what someone else has created?

To all the people who thank me as an inspiration and think positive thoughts about me, thank you! To everyone else who wants something from me and offers me nothing in return, you should really rethink your life path.

Thoughts That Travel to Nowhere
30/Apr/2017 07:37 AM

Do you ever watch yourself think? Are you ever sitting or laying there, doing nothing—thinking and then all of sudden you catch yourself thinking about a specific thought?

What you think is defined by what you have seen and what you have experienced. You cannot think a thought based upon something that is completely out of your realm of reality. You know what you know and that is what you know.

Why you think a thought, however, is decided by you. Yes, thoughts come to all of our minds for reasons we will never full understand, but it is us who decides to think them.

Do you ever find yourself thinking a thought, realize it is not something good for you to be thinking, and stop yourself from thinking it?

The life of a refined person is defined as someone who controls their mind. These are the people who think good thoughts and thereby do good things that cause no damage. The life of an unrefined person is defined as someone who is out of control of their thoughts, their emotions, and their mind. From this, a world of negativity and damage to the individual's own life and to the life of others is given birth to by the thoughts they think.

Everyone understands that the things you do has an impact on the world around you—just as the words you speak has an impact on the world around you. But, where do your actions and your words arise from? The answer to that question is that they arise from the thoughts you think which motivates the actions your take. Thus, all of the life you live, all of the karma you create is given birth to by your thoughts.

What are you thinking? Are you strong enough—are you focused enough—do you care enough to take control over your thoughts?

The Arts Should Have No Judgment
28/Apr/2017 07:33 AM

Most people do not create art. And, I use the term, *"Art,"* to define all aspects of creativity whether it is drawing, painting, sculpting, taking photographs, making music, dancing, doing the martial arts, making films, you name it…

Think back to when you were a child. I'm sure most of us can remember a time when we were busy drawing with crayons or maybe painting with watercolors. What we were doing was whole and perfect onto itself. We loved what we were doing. We didn't judge it. It just made us happy to create. Our parents loved it. It was done by their child and they loved it simply because of that fact—they didn't judge it. Maybe that art work was put away somewhere and you saw it many years later. *"This is what I did!"* Maybe you were a little embarrassed as it was so childlike. But, what happened between the time you drew that crayon drawing and now? What happened is that you decided that you know how art should or should not be. In other words, you became judgmental.

As stated, most people do not create art. Yes, as a child we all did what we did but as adulthood came on, any art development and expression was left behind. Sure, maybe you like a particular brand of music, style of painting, or a certain type of film, but that is what you like—you judged your way to get there. I am sure you have discussed what you like and why you like it with other people. You have probably also put the label of, *"Bad,"* on what you don't like.

All this is fine. It is your right to like what you like and not like what you don't like. But, if you base your life upon a mindset of judgment you are really missing the point. What you are missing is the whole and entire source of and for creativity.

Art is founded in the mind of freedom—of pure expression. It comes from that same place that you embraced as a child when you were drawing with crayons. Free expression; that is the place where all new forms of art are created. That is where contribution and evolution is given birth to in the arts.

So, if all you do is sit around and judge (love or hate) the art created by others, all you are doing is placing a blockade on the road to a better, more whole, freer, and more creative world.

Negative is only negative; it never leads to anything positive. Judgment is only judgment. It is only you actualizing negativity from your mind and sending it into the real world. It never equals anything positive.

So, the next time you find yourself casting judgment, they next time you find yourself being engulfed in the judgment cast by someone else, take control over your mind and remember back to your childhood when art was just art for the sake of art—when you drew or painted or created shapes with Play Doh—remember the purity and the innocence of artistic freedom. Embrace that artistic freedom, put away the judgment, and let art thrive.

The Victim of a Crime
27/Apr/2017 08:07 AM

Have you ever been the victim of a crime? Have you ever had something stolen from your life? Have you ever been hurt by somebody wanting what what you had and then forcefully taking it from you? Have you ever had somebody do something really bad to your life simply because they were only thinking about themselves and not even considering anyone or anything else but themselves?

Have you ever been the perpetrator of a crime? Have you ever stolen something from someone—have you ever hurt somebody? If you have done this, what was your reasoning and what was your justification? Did you think about the person you committed the crime against and what would happen to them in the aftermath of your crime? Did your conscience ever come into play? Did you ever realize you did something wrong and then try to repair the damage you unleashed or did you only continue thinking about yourself? Did you get caught and then make excuses and give justifications for why you did what you did?

Being a victim is painful. Being the perpetrator of a crime may be empowering but if you are walking down that road, if you have committed a crime against someone, what does that say about your moral character?

There are a lot of ways people become the victim of a crime. Certainly, there is personal violence and there is having something stolen from you. These are two of the most obvious forms of crimes.

From a personal level, in my early years I experienced bring on the wrong side of crime. One of the big ones of my early years occurred when a gang descended upon me in a park, stabbed me and took my bike. I still have the scar though it has faded with time. Sure, I had been training in the martial arts for a several years by that point in time but they cut me before I could get off of my bike. Smart street strategy. All that for a bike. That is very sad. But, things like this happen all the time. Then, I got a shot a year or so later. Luckily, it was a small caliber gun, aimed at me from a distance, and it didn't do much damage but I still hold that scar, as well.

During my teenage years I had several radios, 8-Track players, cassette decks, and CBs (remember those?) stolen from my car. It was so upsetting having saved up the money to buy them and then to go down to my car in the morning on my way to school and see I had been robbed. Again, very sad. Small money stolen by a small person.

I've had friends killed. Shot in the head. And, the list goes on… Probably a lot of you out there have similar stories and some may, in fact, have far worse examples. Crime is just sad!

As a creator of things: movies, music, and the like, I have also experienced the crime of the internet. I guess the subtitles of internet crime all came into focus with the whole Napster thing a decade or so back when that, then, start-up company started taking the music created by bands and, *"Sharing it,"* without playing for it. Lars Ulrich of Metallica became the voice of that fight and became highly criticized for his position. But, think about it, if you made your living making music and someone was stealing your livelihood, how would you feel? A crime is a crime!

On the other side of the issue, at this same time period, I remember somebody asked Dave Grohl what he thought. His answer was great, *"I'm already rich, why should I care."* Unfortunately, most of us are not in that financial position so stealing from us on the internet or otherwise does affect our lives.

Perhaps the primary source for crime, whatever that crime may be, is that people do not think about their victims. Especially, if the crime is as easy as freely downloading something from the internet. But, stealing is still stealing. And, someway, someday, somebody will pay.

I get it... I know... Everybody wants everything for free. But, that is just not how the world works!

Moreover, you have to ask yourself, why would you want to steal anybody's creative anything anyway? Why can't you create your own some-thing.

Currently, there is this whole false belief about, *"Fair Use,"* out there in the realms of cyberspace right now. I've even seen a few things written about the subject on-line. But, who ever wrote those pieces is writing for a captive audience—they are telling people what they want to hear. For someone who has personally walked down that road in court, I can tell you, without a doubt, there is no such things as Fair Use. The moment a person makes one penny based upon something someone else created they are in violation of the law. If they hurt a person's existence, even in the smallest of ways, by stealing something someone else created they are in violation of the law.

That's what a copyright is, somebody created something, they own that something, and you can't use that something unless they allow you to use it. If you take it from them without asking that is stealing. Don't believe me, ask an attorney who practices copyright law.

But, what is the law? Did the law ever catch the people who stabbed me in order to steal my bike way back when? No. Did the guy who shot me ever get caught for that? No. Did I ever get any of my radios back? No. So, I was the one left without do to somebody taking something from me.

If you have ever had a crime happen to you, did the person get caught and go to jail? I hope so. But... In many cases, that is not what happens.

Now, I am certain that the people who live the lifestyle of committing crimes do eventually end up in jail because sooner or later they will get caught. But, what they did to me and to all the other people they victimized was not healed in that process as we were simply the ones left without.

And, I think this all goes to the basis and the motivation for crime—people do things because they do not think about anyone else but themselves. They do things because they do not care about anyone else but themselves. If they are caught, they try to turn the blame onto the person they were victimizing and/or onto someone or anyone but themselves.

But, they committed a crime! They took something from someone that damaged that someone's life! And, that is just wrong!

So, do you ever commit crimes? Do you ever steal things in the real world or in cyberspace? If you do, you are a criminal and you are doing something wrong that is hurting someone. Maybe you will get away with it, at least for the moment. But, what you are doing is not right. Can you open your eyes? Can you care enough about the greater good of the world to stop it? Can you care enough to stop justifying your actions? Can you care enough about the person you are stealing from or hurting to stop what you are doing? And, if you have committed a crime against someone can you care enough to go back and fix what you have broken?

If you have even been the victim of a crime, and I hope you have not, but then you know how it feels. Let that be your motivating factor for you not being a criminal.

Most of us are good people. We think about what will be the impact of what we are doing on the lives of other people before we do anything? Do you? Or, do you not care?

There is nothing anyone can do to anyone to make a person care. But, you can choose to care. From the small things to the big things, you do not have to be a criminal.

*　　*　　*
26/Apr/2017 07:17 PM

If you lie: to get what you want, make yourself look like something more, or to receive sympathy you can never call anyone else a liar when they lie to you and damage your life.

Changing Time Changing Culture
26/Apr/2017 07:16 AM

As you get older in life you gain perspective. You begin to see how things were different <u>then</u> compared to how they are <u>now</u>. ...How certain things that were once considered acceptable have changed and now they are taboo.

This goes both ways. In my early years, during the 1960s and into the 1970s, culture began to free up. Things that were once unacceptable became okay. Sexual morality opened up; people could have guilt free sex. The accepted rights of the female gender, the various races, and of gay cultural became the norm and so forth...

Over the more recent decades, however, certain elements of our culture have begun to shift the opposite direction. For example, you constantly hear in the news there are so many people being fired, sued, and chastised for sexual impropriety. With the expanding mindset of what is considered right and what is considered wrong that definition has become monetized and people seek methods to bring down the life of people they do not like based upon what they allegedly said or did. Then, they expect to be paid. Certainly, doing something to someone that they do not want done to them is bad. But again, this goes to cultural programming and how an individual was trained.

For example, you commonly hear of teachers, both male and female, going to jail due to the fact that they had consensual sex with a student. The TV Show *South Park* did a very funny episode about this subject a few years back. Now, I'm not talking about some old dude overpowering some young kid, either physically or psychological, what I am talking about is choice. When I was in high school it was not uncommon for teachers to go out with students. Yeah, it seemed a little weird, like why would she be going out with that old guy... In fact, I had a couple of my female friends who were going out with guys deep in their thirties. But, for the high school guys who hooked up with a female teacher, everybody was in full-on approval.

Again, this all goes to the time in history. And, I believe that this is where a lot of these problems arise. A person, groomed at a specific point in history, comes away with a set of morals based upon that time in history. They believe what they were taught to believe—their knowledge was gained from what they experienced. A younger person, who has been shaped by a completely different set of morals and understandings, simply operates from a different set of standards. And, if these two people cannot find a common ground, then problems will arise.

There is not a whole or total right and wrong when it comes to interpersonal relationships. All we have is what we were taught and what we've experienced. From this, some of us try to evolve and become better and more understanding people, while others hold fast to what they were taught at they time they were taught it.

I think it is really important to keep this in mind whenever you cast your judgment in the direction of one person or another. People are shaped by the culture of the time they exist within. Many times, people mean no harm, they are just expressing their understanding of life to a person who was schooled from a completely different perspective.

Interpersonal understanding comes from understanding.

Zen Filmmaking: The Good, The Bad, and The People That Don't Know What the Fuck They're Talking About
25/Apr/2017 06:19 PM

Ever since the inception of Zen Filmmaking, that was heralded with the release of *The Roller Blade Seven*, people have contacted me about my method of filmmaking. In the early days, it was largely via letters but soon after that everybody climbed onto the internet and then everybody had a lot to say.

There have been a lot of people, over the years, who have actually contacted me and questioned, how do I do what I do. Those are the people I respect. Love my films or hate my films, they are the ones who cared enough to ask me what was actually going on. They came to the source and inquired. And, going to the source is the only way to gain true knowledge.

Some of these people contacted me because they wanted to follow the path of Zen Filmmaking. That's great! Make it your own…

Early in my filmmaking career, (which you have to keep in mind did not begin until I was thirty-two years old so I had a lot of life-experience prior to that), I also began to see people coming to conclusions about what I did, how I did it, and why I did it. These discourses where then mostly entered into magazines that discussed the low budget, no budget, and cult level of filmmaking. In some cases, they got it right. But, in many, (in fact most), cases they were simply wrong. Yet, these people had a pulpit and from that pulpit they broadcasted their thoughts about Zen Filmmaking, Zen Films, and me out to the world.

As a professional researcher, I always found this method to be suspect, as these people were simply discussing their feelings that were not based in fact. Yet, they were presenting their opinions, observations, and speculations as if they were fact. This is truly the wrong way to put forward information to the world and this mindset is what has given birth to the whole culture of, *"Fake News,"* we are currently living within—as from these inaccurate depictions further counterfactual statements and misunderstandings are given birth to. People heard, *"This,"* and, thus, they believed, *"That."* But, it is all based on bullshit. It is all based on somebody putting what they think they know out there but they do not have the true facts as they have not done any actual research. I know… I get it… Research is hard to do. It is time-consuming and it often costs money. It is so much easier to just read or hear something and then believe what you want to believe. But, the fact is, if you want to know the truth about a subject, (any subject), research is the only way to arrive at a factual and valid conclusion. And, you must enter into any research gathering with an open mind and not use it as simply a way to justify what you <u>think</u> you already know.

  Personally, in virtually all of the aforementioned cases, I found the discourses to be amusing. But, that's just who I am. I easily poke fun at myself. If they weren't flat out defamatory lies or someone making money off of one of my creations when they had no responsibility for its actualization, I was good.

  On the larger scale, I have always wondered why do people do this? Why do people want to spread their feelings about something or someone and, moreover, why do they want to transmit something out to the world when what they are saying is not based in fact but is solely based upon personal opinion, second-hand knowledge, and/or speculation? Sure, I understand, most people like something or someone for some nondescript reason but that reason is generally based upon them not possessing a true understanding about anything. Thus, what does that reason for like or dislike truly mean? Do you ever think about that when you form your opinions and from your opinions make your judgments which leads to your statements?

As Zen Filmmaking is a defined form of filmmaking, many people have also taken aim at the craft. They have taken aim at it but all they know about it is that in Zen Filmmaking we do not use a script. But, there is a lot more to it than that. And no, Zen Filmmaking is not just about showing up somewhere and seeing what happens next. So, if you've heard that, if you've believed that, if you've rebroadcast that, YOU ARE WRONG!

Also, there have been a lot of people who have seen *Roller Blade Seven* or some clips from it and decided that was the epitome of Zen Filmmaking and all of my films are just like RB7. The fact is, a lot of people don't get what Donald G. Jackson and I were trying to do with *The Roller Blade Seven* and they hate it. I get it! That movie is weird! If you don't like weird movies you probably will hate it. But, think about this, we made that movie over twenty-five years ago—whatever you think about it: love it or hate; we did something right because people are still discussing it.

On a more personal note, occasionally I have seen some people say, *"Scott Shaw makes shitty movies,"* and stuff like that. Okay… That's what you think… But, how many of my movies have you actually seen? Many people make this comment after only seeing maybe *Roller Blade Seven* or *Max Hell Frog Warrior.* I have made a lot of movies! Honestly, how many of them have you seen? Have you seen any of my documentaries? Have you seen any of my music videos? Have you followed my filmmaking evolution and watched any of my Non-Narrative Zen Films, my Zen Film Art Captures, my Zen Film Movies in the Moment, or my Zen Film Mind Rides? If you haven't, then you have no idea what I'm doing. Moreover, if you have not read my written words on the subject of filmmaking, if you have not seen my interviews, if you have not met me, again, you are basing your opinion on a preconceived notion that you have no factual bases to possess. Love my movies, hate my movies, I get it… But, if you haven't seen my films, if you don't know my philosophy about filmmaking, if you have not actually spoken to me, then how can you judge anything?

And, this goes to the whole point of this piece… Sure, you're just a screen name out there in the nowhere of cyberspace. You will never have to pay for your cyber crimes. But, no matter what moniker you use, you should be whole enough to know the facts about what you're talking about before you ever spew your misunderstandings out to the world. In other words, BE MORE. For me, that is the key to life. That is how the people who have truly excelled and made a contribution to the world have done it. Care enough to care. Learn the true facts. Go to the source and ask before you speak. Be more than someone who talks about someone else, go out there and create your own something.

What Happens If You Die Today?
24/Apr/2017 03:10 PM

People spend much of the lifetime thinking about what they want to do. This is especially the case in the early years of a person's life. It is the common belief that when you are young the options are many and there will be time to achieve them. But, as one passes through life they quickly learn that the achievement of what they want takes effort and all of sudden, there you are, too old to do what you thought you could do.

People find solace in rooting for a team, loving a band, or waiting for the next comic book in a series to be revealed. Though all of these things distract one from the realities of life, personal achieve was and has always been the goal. Are you moving towards the achievement of anything by rooting for a team, loving a band, or waiting for a comic book?

People want to be and to do something. But, being and doing are never easy. Being and doing begin by being and doing. Most people never understand this, thus the set about on a life course of witnessing what others are being or doing. From this, is born the armchair quarterback. The person who sits by themselves or with friends and analysis or criticizes what other are being or doing.

People want to become but they do not have the focused energy to become. Thus, they find talking about those who have become is an easy antidote. But, all this does is to distract the mind from what once was the desired end goal; becoming.

People want to be something, people want to do something, people want to receive acclamations for what they have done but when they have done nothing how can they receive anything?

People want. But, wanting is not doing. What do you want? What are doing to achieve it? If you died today what legacy will you leave behind?

Can I Ever Forgive You?
24/Apr/2017 02:56 PM

Have you ever had somebody do something bad to you—something that really messed with your life? How did that feel? Pretty bad, I would imagine.

Why did they do it?

In some cases, people do things because they actually want to hurt the life of another person. In other cases, they did what they because they were only thinking about themselves and how what they were doing would make their what-ever better. Sometimes people are simply unaware of what they are doing. They are living in a space of interpersonal unconsciousness, not thinking about anyone else but themselves, so when what they do hurts another person they are not even aware of the pain they are inflicting.

No matter what the cause, somebody did something bad to you—it negatively affected your life, and you are the one left dealing with the aftermath.

When the facts are presented to them, the culprit in these matters oftentimes justifies, lies, and denies what they have done. Though they justify, lie, and deny, it was them who instigated the entire situation by doing some-thing that affected some-one. They did what they did, it was them who instigated the action, but it is you who is left dealing with the consequences.

In all of our lives, when these situations occur, we are the one who has had our life devastated and due to the fact that the negative situation was more than likely orchestrated by a particular individual, we are also the one forced to continually think about the person who did what they did to us. Thus, this compounds the injury as we must not only try to fix what happened to our life but we must remember a person that we most likely never wanted to know in the first place.

This is a strange equation if you think about it... You didn't want a situation to happen to you. You didn't ask for it to happen to you. But, some-body, did some-thing bad to you and you are the one forced to not only think about the situation but about the person, as well, as you are the only one left dealing with the consequences.

In many cases, the person who performed the negative deed never thinks about their victim(s) at all. If they get caught, they may think about themselves—they may justify why they did what they did. They may even believe what they did was right. But, if any-thing any-one does hurts any-body they are the only one at fault. But, most people never even think about the negative impact what they did had on the life of the person that encountered what they have done. Some people even take pride in what they have done and do it again. Perhaps this goes to the source of the problem, as the instigator rarely apologizes to the person they victimized. Moreover, even fewer people, if any, ever think about how they can repair the damage that they have unleashed.

From this, what is born is a victim locked into a state of mental agitation and a culprit moving through their life while, most likely, hurting others. I think we can all agree; this is not good.

Some would say, *"Just forgive."* Though that is a nice catchphrase, forgiveness is very hard if your life has become defined by the damage another person has instigated. Thus, how can you ever forgive?

Some people who have been victimized attempt forgiveness, stating, "God will get them and make them pay." And, the fact is, that generally does come to pass. If a person is saying negative and judgmental things or if they are doing things that injure the lives of other people, they will eventually pay the price as what they are saying or doing brings negativity their direction. But, if you've been hurt, you've been hurt. Though you may be able to philosophize your way out of the damage in your own mind (and this is not a bad thing) most people, all they are left with is attempting to chart a new life defined by the damage unleashed on them by the hands of another person. Thus, forgiveness or even forgetting is out of the question.

Some people claim revenge is what must occur. But, in many cases, particularly in this modern world, revenge is almost impossible. And, in fact, even if you did get revenge it may make you feel a little bit bitter but will it actually undo what was done to your life? Probably not. This is the same with karma... Sure, a person may, *"Get theirs,"* but how does them, *"Getting theirs,"* fix what they did to your life?

And, here lies the sourcepoint of the problem... No matter what you do, no matter how you feel about what was done to you, no matter what thoughts you have about the person who did it to you, it will only be you who is left to deal with the aftermath.

As many of us will encounter damage brought to our life by the words and the deeds of another person during our lifetime, there is no clear route to forgiveness or requital. At best, all we have is the ability to make a conscious effort to repair our life once damage has been done to it. How do we do that? The answer to that is different for each situation. And, there is no universal cure.

Certainly, things can be halted before they are unleashed. If we see someone saying or doing bad or negative things, sprouting words or doing deeds that will hurt someone/anyone, we can tell them to stop. In fact, it is our responsibility to do just that. And, that may block some negative deeds from being unleashed. Also, if someone is taking pride in their negative action(s), we can tell them that they should be ashamed of themselves for hurting the life of someone/anyone. But, will they care? Most people do not care about anyone enough to care that they may be hurting someone—especially if they do not personally know that individual. This is particularly the case in the age of the internet where the only thing people are is a vague screen name off somewhere in the distance of cyberspace. They never have to go face-to-face with the person they are hurting and backup what they have done. Thus, many feel they can say or do anything they want and get away with it. All of us with a conscience know this is wrong. But, look around, it goes on all the time.

Do you ever question, *"How will what I am doing or what I am saying affect someone else?"* If you don't, if you don't care about the answer, or if you actually want your words or your deeds to hurt someone else, again, here lies the root of the problem.

Ultimately, all life begins with you. You should only do good things. You should only say good things. You should never be critical, nor should you ever judge. You should think about other people and not only think about yourself. For all unconscious, unthinking, uncaring activity does is to damage the lives of other people and, thus, sets a course of events in motion in your own life where though you may be adrenalized in your moment of conquest, you will be on the receiving end of life-damage in the not too distant future. If you live in a world of unleashed negativity, you have defined your own reality. What do you think you will encounter if you perform negative actions and speak negative words?

If someone does something bad to you, can you ever forgive them? I don't know? Maybe... Maybe not... But, what you need to do is create a world around you where all you are doing is saying and doing good things. Then, at least, if someone says or does something bad to you or about you, the positivity of your life will continue to be the primary defining factor of your existence while the other person's own negativity will come to be the defining factor of their life. And, we all know who wins and ultimately comes out on top in those situations.

Don't hurt people. If you have hurt someone, fix it. Choose to make the world a better place.

The Availability of Your Choices
24/Apr/2017 08:29 AM

Your life is defined by the choices you make predicated upon what is available to you. But, what is available to you is defined by your understanding of availability.

You can only make a choice from the options you have. But, how many options are out there that you do not know about?

A very simply example of this understanding is, you want to go and eat dinner at a restaurant. You know about a few restaurants that are open in your area. So, you will make the choice about where you will eat defined by your knowledge that these particular restaurants are in business. But, what about the restaurants you do not know about? Maybe there are several of them, very close to you, that you did not realize are in existence. Maybe you would like the food at these restaurants better but as you do not know that they are in existence you cannot go to them as they are not on your list of choices. Thus, your opinions have been limited by your understanding of availability.

Your life is defined by the choices you make within the parameters of what is available to you. Most people limit their choices by their lack of understanding of availability. They do this because they close themselves off from looking to the greater understanding. They do this because the lock themselves into a mindset of believe that they know all that they need to know. They do this because they base their availability judgment on ego, defined by believing that what they know is right and what you think is wrong.

How often have you witnessed a person making a choice that they believed was their only option but you knew that they had so many more opportunities open to them if they would just open their eyes? One person can look at another person and question why they do not look beyond what they believe is available to them. But, at best, this would simply be another method of casing judgment based upon personal understanding. Because what a person believes is what a person believe and here lies the entire problem with the birth of availability.

People do what they do based upon what they currently know. Few people ever look outside of what they already think they know to find new levels of knowledge and understanding, thereby leading them to a new set of available options. Thus, most people live an entire life trapped by what they already think that they know.

There is more out there. There are great options out there. You do have additional choices to make but you must first look beyond what you think you know and explore a new level of availability.

Your choices are defined by what you believe is available to you. Expand your options and a whole new world of choice is revealed.

Empathy: Self Awareness Through Caring
22/Apr/2017 09:21 AM

I was just going to begin writing a piece about empathy for a journal, detailing how it is a refined level of human consciousness and how some people never actually mentally mature to the degree where they actually care about another person and embrace this ideology. Then, last night, I was flipping channels and I came upon a documentary, *Burn Motherfucker Burn,* defining the riots that took place in Los Angeles in 1965 and 1992; what lead up to them, and their aftermath. It was a very good documentary that truly provided insight into the mindset of the people and what was their motivations for doing what they did.

To give a little bit of a backstory here, for those of you who do not know about my personal history, I was part and parcel to both of the riots. In 1965 I was a young boy living in Southcentral L.A. In the documentary they discuss how it was a locked community, virtually wholly African-American, as the people either could not or did not feel comfortable moving outwards from their neighborhood. Within this community there was a lot of inequality and frustration. I totally witnessed that. I was literally the only Caucasian any-body at my grammar school. In the documentary you also see how much of the black populous of the area hated whites and were out to get them at any opportunity. I too experienced that. I mean there was one time when nine or ten teenagers descended upon me when I was eight years old. And, that was not the only time I encountered this style of behavior. I think most of us would ask, *"What kind of person would do something like that?"* But, in the documentary you can listen and see the rage of the people of the area.

Now, this is not a, *"Oh Boo Hoo,"* moment on my part. But, what it does is provide an initial glimpse into peering into the mind of a person who does not possess empathy. They are locked into a mindset of, "Me against them," "Kill or be killed." From this, no level of higher consciousness can ever be found. And, in fact, if you were to mention this to a person who embraces this mindset they would not even care. From this, we can instantly see how some people have the capacity to develop empathy where others, for whatever reason, do not.

When the riots broke out in 1965 it was a scary time. People in the documentary describe it as such. Tanks and troop carriers drove up and down the streets, along with a lot of highly armed National Guard and police. Think about being a white person living in that environment. As was documented, many people of the community went out stealing and destroying the buildings using Molotov cocktails. That was the first time I heard the expression, *"Burn Baby Burn."* But, what did these people achieve? Ultimately, all they did was to destroyed their own community.

Again, we see a mindset guided by adrenalin and motivated anger. But, what is the ultimate outcome of living a life based upon those emotions. Perhaps a half a century later the people who took part in this event can look back with pride at the actions that took but how does any of that help the greater good? How does it make anything better? How does any of that help anyone?

The documentary then went into discussing the aftermath of the 1965 L.A. riots and how what came to be known as, "Bussing," later came into practice in Los Angeles as a method to integrate the communities. What, "Bussing," meant was that they randomly chose school-aged children from areas like Southcentral L.A., Watts, and Compton, put them on busses, and drove them to schools in other areas of the city. At the time, I was living in what is now known as Koreatown. There came to be a number of students bussed to the junior high school, (now middle school), I was attending. In some cases, I made fast friends with those who arrived on the bus. As I had spent my early years growing up in a neighborhood not different from their own, we had a basis for interaction. In other case, I witnessed how some of the people were simply in the early stages of becoming a hardened thug and they brought violence along with them. Some of these people hurt a lot of the local residence. Eventually, this program was scrapped.

Viewing the two levels of interactive consciousness, possessed by these people who were brought into a new community, we can see the different pathways of personal evolution. Some people are nice, they want a better world for themselves and others, while others harbor hatred and embrace the negative. From this, all that is given birth to is external and personal destruction.

A person shapes their mind and who they are to become at two critical stages of their life. The first is early childhood. At this stage, one is guided towards who they are to become primarily by family and cultural interactions. The second stage occurs during adolescence. At this stage a person begins to shape who they are to become by social interactions and choices made about how they want to be seen by the world and what they hope to achieve, defined by what opportunities are available to them. If a person is wholly embraced with a mindset of only thinking about self and about their own perceived personal tragedy, they can never move beyond that mindset. From this, no empathy will ever be found within that individual.

The second riot that was discussed in the documentary was the 1992 L.A. riot and what lead up to it. As discussed in the documentary, the images of Rodney Kind being beaten by the police will forever be remembered. Then, these officers initially being found innocent of their crime set the community ablaze.

I personally had a curious interaction with this riot. I was filming *Samurai Vampire Bikers from Hell*. We were scheduled to do a night shoot in West Hollywood and

Chinatown the evening the riot began. I live in the South Bay area of L.A. and as I left for the shoot during traffic time I decided to take the streets to L.A. Having grown up in Southcentral I often drive through the area as kind of a remembrance. I actually drove right through the intersection where the riot began. In the news reports I later watched there was a short time between the initial inception and when everything actually broke off when the participants had dispersed. For some cosmic reason that is when I passed through the area. I though there had just been an accident or something. But, I was lucky, if you see the documentary there were a lot of people screaming that they were going to kill white people and we all saw what happened to the unsuspecting white truck driver Reginald Denny. That was very sad.

Me, I drove on, completely unaware of how the city was erupting, to the location. If you've seen the movie, that's the night we filmed the escalator scene at the Beverly Center, the point when the character McGavin stakes Lord Toronomo outside in DTLA, and when we filmed some of the stuff in Chinatown.

We were on our way to another location but I kept getting paged by my lady. 911! Pagers, remember those? Anyway, I stopped at a pay phone (remember those?) and called her. *"There's a riot going on,"* she exclaimed. With that we ended the shoot for the evening.

I listened to the news on the radio as I began to drive home and as there were snipers shooting at cars along the 110, (the freeway I would normally take home from Hollywood), I went out and around taking the 101 North out to the valley and then the 405 South home. As I came down over the hill, I could see the city was burning.

In the documentary, they interview people like singer Perry Farrell (Jane's Addiction). He spoke about how he had just bought a house in Venice but had no furniture. With the riot going on and everybody looting, he went out, and his house became fully furnished. He said he had a great time. How pathetic is that! A white guy who can afford to <u>buy</u> a house in Venice stealing. That is just wrong.

Again, all this goes to the mindset of empathy and higher consciousness.

You can destroy. You can steal. You can blame it on whatever you want to blame it on—whatever you've gone through but whatever <u>you</u> do is whatever <u>you</u> do. You are doing it! You are making a choice to do it! And, this is where the definition of a person of conscience and/or consciousness comes into play.

Do you do what you do knowing it is wrong? Do you do what you do not even caring if it is right or wrong? Do you do what you do not caring who it may negativity affect? If you do injure someone or something, do you care or do you only present yourself as the victim? Here lies the question of empathy. Are you more than what you personally are feeling?

Empathy means understanding and caring about another/other people. Empathy means becoming consciously interactive with another person. Empathy means that you are self-aware enough to actually embrace, understand, and consciously feel what someone else is experiencing. But, to do this you have to be whole enough onto yourself to care enough to care—you have to understand that you are not the only person who feels. You have to be completely enough, in yourself, to not base your entire existence upon what you want, how you want to feel, how you sense that you are perceived by the other, and how you can get back at those you feel have wronged you.

Empathy is a refined level of human consciousness. Some people naturally embrace it. Some people do not. Whatever the case is with you, you can choose to care. You can choose to allow yourself to be less and allow someone else to be more. You can seek to understand instead of casting judgment. You can rise from the lower levels of your inner self and embrace humanity and give back instead of simply unleashing destruction and either taking pride in your actions or denying them.

Empathy is you turning you off and you becoming interactive with the larger, greater, better all.

Don't hurt. Don't destroy. Care enough to care. It begins with you.

Judging Enlightenment
21/Apr/2017 08:08 AM

Recently, there was a guy on Dr. Phil's show that claimed he was enlightened but his wife wasn't happy with his behavior as he had spent all their money and lost their business so Dr. Phil surprised the guest and had Deepak Chopra come on to analyze and rate this man's level of enlightenment and/or whether or not he was actually enlightened at all. Chopra's determination was that the man still had too many self-involved traits to be enlightened. Though he said what he said about the man in a very politically correct manner.

Now, I am paraphrasing here as I did not watch the entire episode—as I do not watch that style of TV but I caught the highlights online. There is a problem with all of this is, however. That problem is, who is anybody to judge anyone's level of enlightenment? ...Even Deepak Chopra. Not to mention would a person who was enlightened claim to be enlightened? No. That's ego. That's not enlightenment.

Before I get a bit deeper into this, let me say, most people do not care about enlightenment. They spend none of their Life-Time pursing refined spirituality, consciousness, or the pathway to enlightenment. Yet, there have been and there are millions of people, throughout the centuries, who have focused their entire life on this achievement. But, here is the problem, people mistaking see enlightenment as something. This is where all of the problems on the pathway and/or analysis of enlightenment begin.

For example, the guy who claimed enlightenment used all of the catch phrases, rising from this chakra up to that one, and so on. This is all bullshit. All of the psychobabble mumbo-jumbo that goes on in association with enlightenment is what keeps anyone from actually obtaining enlightenment. It all leads one down the road of Maya, (illusion). There is no pathway to enlightenment.

There is no technique that will get you there. As such, describing your pathway to your obtainment it just demonstrates a complete lack of true understanding.

Now, onto the judgment thereof...

Chopra is of East Indian descent, a medical doctor, and he has written a lot of books about higher consciousness. He has made a great contribution to the raising understanding of interpersonal human consciousness. Okay... But, he is not the all-knowing expert on enlightenment. No one is. He is a media personality. If he were solely walking the road to his own enlightenment, he would not be in the public eye or on TV whatsoever. He would only be focused on embracing his *Sadhana* (spiritual practice). In fact, simply by agreeing to discuss this subject alerts one to the fact that Copra, himself, is not enlightened. Though I am certain that he would claim that he is.

In Zen Buddhism it is understood that we all are enlightened, we have simply forgotten this fact. And, like I always say, *"Enlightenment is easy. It's life that's hard."*

But, back to the central point of this conversation, people misunderstand enlightenment because they think of it as a thing—an accomplishment—a something out there that is nearly impossible to achieve but you may get there via some highly specific intricate technique. The problem is, each school of philosophic thought has a different pathway to its obtainment. If is was one thing, located in one place, then there would be one way to get there.

Enlightenment is not something out there. Nor is it even a state of mind. Enlightenment simply, *"Is,"* when you let yourself embrace it. Thus, the enlightened person never goes around claiming, *"I am enlightened,"* and the pundit never judges whether or not someone else is or is not enlightened.

If you are, you are. If you're not, you're not.

Just BE and you will SEE.

The Truth As You Think You Know It
20/Apr/2017 07:52 AM

Most people are not trained lawyers, psychologists, sociologists, martial artists, or any other profession that takes a lot of years of schooling to master. Most people have never played professional football, basketball, baseball—they've never acted in a high budget Hollywood movie or TV Show nor have they made a feature film. Most people have never lived with the indigenous people of South Asia, the Middle East, or South America. Yet, everybody believes they know what they know—they believe what they believe—then they tell others what they believe and that false-knowledge, (that fake news), is put out there as if it were fact. From this, other people hear it, believe it, and the lie is spread farther and farther.

What do you think that type of life-action does to the rest of the world? What contribution do you think it makes? What do you think saying things, based upon unsubstantiated knowledge, does to you as an evolving human being and to the rest of the world?

Where does knowledge come from? True knowledge comes from undertaking a long course of study involving the facts of a particular subject. But, is this where most people gain their knowledge? No, it is not. Where do most people get their knowledge? They get it from what they read, what they hear, what they want to believe, what makes them feel good when they hear it, and what they think they already know. But, that is not knowledge. As best, that is opinion being disguised as knowledge.

An opinion is nothing more than a false belief nurtured by what and/or whom a person chooses to listen to. Thus, if a person or a large group of people follow a path of belief based upon opinion, a world is born where a person's life evolution and the greater scheme of Life Goodness is harmed by what a person thinks that they know. ...Because what they know is not the truth. It is simply spoken opinion.

What do you believe? Who or what do you believe in? What course of study did you undertake to provide you with a valid frame of references for the beliefs that you cast on life events and/or people? What research did you do to provide you with a factual basis for speaking the words you speak? What makes you believe you have the right to say anything based upon judgment?

Whatever you say, particular in this age of the internet, has the potential to have wide spanning affect. This is why many people say things: they want their beliefs to be believed—they want to get famous due to their beliefs. And, this can be done. But, the question has to be asked, "At what cost?" What cost to you and your karma for judging someone or something else and what cost to the world who listens to your words and believes them when they are not based upon truth only personal or self-motivated belief?

As I frequently say, *"The whole world begins with you."* What you say and what you do sets your ultimate destiny into motion. This occurs because what you say and what you do does not only affect you but it affects everyone who hears your words and/or comes into contact with you. But, most people never think about this. They just think what they think about a person based upon whatever psychologically motivated logic they follow—they just believe what they believe about an external world event based upon what they were programmed into believing. What very few people ever do is to study the facts of a situation, go to its roots, and actually come away with True Knowledge based upon appropriate study instead of simply unleashing an opinion based on opinionated limited understanding that has been disguised as the truth.

Just because somebody says something does not make it the truth. Do you have the personal Self-Awareness to understand this fact?

Your words have power. Most people know this but they do not truly think about this. Most, only use what they say to guide others to believe what they believe—not based upon fact but solely upon their judgmental, self-motivated, opinion. And, this is a problem.

If we look at the modern world, it is obvious that most people do not care about the greater good. They do not care about putting their own beliefs on hold long enough to study the True Facts of Reality before they spout out what they think, based on what they heard and chose to believe, and, thus, what they hope others will think. But, as in all cases in life, the betterment of humanity begins with one person doing one good thing—one person putting their own ego on hold, learning the true facts, caring about a person or person(s), and doing what is best for The All based upon the factual acquired knowledge they have obtained.

Are you strong enough to stop judging and spreading your opinion as fact? Are you tough enough to stop attempting to hurt other people with your words or actions? Are you whole enough to stop attempting to make others believe what you have heard and want them to believe? Are you intelligent enough to actually become schooled in a subject to the degree where you can actually participate in that field on a professional level? Or, do you not care about anybody but who you care about—the world be damned, and you are going to go about saying what you are saying, doing what you are doing, no matter who or what it hurts and what catastrophe it unleashes?

Conscious evolution, on the personal or the global level, is based upon true acquired knowledge. From this, True Knowledge grows and the world and all its people are made better and more whole.

What do you say? What do you do? What do you base your knowledge and beliefs upon? How does that affect your life? And, how does that affect the world as a whole? You should think about his before you speak.

You Did It. It's Your Fault.
13/Apr/2017 07:43 AM

I always find one of the most curious things about life is how people <u>do something</u>; they create a situation but when it does not turn out the way they want it to turn out or the situation they instigated damages some-thing or the life of some-one then they attempt to hide from the fact that they are the one who instigated the occurrence in the first place. And, in fact, attempt to be seen as the victim in the entire ploy. …Let alone they do not take any responsibility for what they have done and attempt to undo or repair it.

Why is this? Why are people so self-involved, self-serving, and uncaring? Why do people only think about themselves? Why do they appear to be the victim when they are the one who instigated the entire everything in the first place?

I think if we studied the life of each person we would find a very individualized reason for why a person does what they do. That's what psychologists do all the time—dig deeply into a person's why. But, at the core of what sets any situation sideways is the fact that one person only thought about themselves—their needs, their desires. They did not think about how what they did would or could affect anyone else.

We live in an interesting time where, especially here in the free world, people are encouraged to be themselves—to feel what they feel and do what they do in the most open manner possible. But, there is a problem with this. That problem is that many people have never developed an internal sense of right and wrong. They have never mentally developed themselves to the degree where they look outside of themselves and question how what they do will affect the everything else. They just think. They just feel. They just desire. They just judge. They just react. From this is born the world of pain and suffering. Perhaps not the pain and suffering of the instigator but the pain and suffering of all those who were forced deal with what was done—what was instigated by someone else.

This is where the concept of discrimination come into play. There was an elemental text written on this subject by the great Hindu Sage, Sri Shachara Charya, titled, *Vivekachudamani* or *The Crest jewel of Discrimination.* I often recommend this text for it truly teaches the aspirant how to take the focus off of Self and place it upon the Higher Self. I also recommend certain translations of the *Tao Te Ching* for this same reason. But, it seems that nobody wants to read these books. Nobody wants to take conscious control over their mind. Sure, everybody wants to be richer, prettier, more powerful, more famous, you name it… But, no one wants to care about the Higher Self—about giving instead of taking—about thinking before reacting. It seems that no one wants to control the beast within. They just want to let the beast run free doing whatever it wants to do. But then, something goes wrong… Then, they hurt something. Then, they hurt someone. Instead of caring enough to care, they bob and weave but never look at themselves and their responsibility for unleashing the life situation.

Do you ever think about what you think? Do you ever think about why you think it? Do you ever think about how your emotions control you? Do you ever think about why you let your emotions control you? Do you ever think about what actions emulate from you because of what you think and how you are emotionally reacting to the world?

Studying yourself is not difficult. When you take a walk by yourself what do you think about? When you are taking a walk by yourself this is a really good time to perform a mental exercise. Study what you are thinking. When you are alone do you think solely about yourself—what you want, who you want, who you want to hurt, how you want to feel? Or, do you think about someone else? Do you ponder how you can make the life of another person or the whole world better? There is no right or wrong answer to this mental exercise. It is just a simple experiment where you can learn about you.

All things in this life start with one person. Whether these things are big or small, bad or good, there is one person who instigated what came next.

Who are you in the instigations that you instigate? Are you a small person who focuses your instigations solely on selfish motives, thinking only about yourself? Do you focus your instigations on other people, on doing things that affect other people and then scream, *"It wasn't me..."* Or, *"Whoa is me,"* when your actions hurt someone else?

Do you think before you do? Do you look to the future? Chart what may happen next if you do this or if you do that? Do you first study yourself, learn what are your motivations, control the beast within, and then do only what can help instead of hurt?

Honestly, you know if what you are saying is helpful or hurtful. Honestly, you know if what you are doing is good or bad. Honestly, you know that taking things that are not yours is bad—doing things that cause other people pain is bad—saying words that have the potential to hurt someone is bad—being judgment, vain, or emotionally out of control is bad. You know what is bad! Just as you know what is good. Why do you do anything bad?

There are a lot of people in this modern world that are seriously emotionally out of control. Have you ever met one of them? They are the most self-involved, unaware, reactionary people you will ever meet. Yet, they constantly can come up with an excuse for why they are behaving badly. Maybe they even believe these excuses themselves. Maybe that is what actually makes the emotionally out of control. Maybe that is why they don't get psychiatric help. Maybe...

Then, there are the aware, the educated, the successful... They have achieved what they have achieved but they too do things that set bad occurrences into motion in other people's lives. What is their excuse? It is the same excuse. It is the same justification. It is the same logic and reason—they didn't think about anyone or anything else first.

What do you do before you do? Do you contemplate what you are about to do? If you don't, you are a selfish, unthinking person. That is just the way it is. But, you can be more. But, you have to choose to be more. Do you choose to be more? If you do, then be more! Think about others first. Put your own desires and emotions aside before you do anything. Study yourself. Study your reason why. Control yourself. And, make the world a better place rather than just dodging any responsibility after you have done what you have done.

A Gentleman Smiles and Walks Away
10/Apr/2017 07:34 AM

I was in the supermarket this afternoon, picking up dinner. I was walking past the meat department and this guy, in his mid-forties, just totally goes off on this elderly woman. *"I said I was sorry, that should be enough for you, you old bat,"* he exclaims. *"You probably are all alone in life and you have no one!"* Then, he storms off down the aisle. Wow… What was that?

Apparently, he had cut in on the lady trying to grab a package of meat and she said something to him. Now, first of all, we all understand that the elderly can be a little testy at times. That's just who they are. You don't confront them about it. But, more over, a gentleman never behaves in that manner. What is so important that you need to treat another person, old or young, like that? A gentleman smiles and walks away.

I believe that we have probably all encountered people like this: rude, arrogant, judgmental, and demeaning of other people. But, where does that type of behavior arise? It comes from the mind of an insecure person; for anyone who insults anybody for any reason does so from a mindset of insecurity. Why? Because if a person is whole and secure onto themselves they do not need to judge anybody's anything. It is only the weak minded who behave in this manner.

Moreover, what a person says about another person, in moments like this, is what they truly think about themselves. The insecure and the unaware find a method to project their own fears out to humanity. As they are so out of control of their own mind and out of tune with their true inner self all they can embrace in the lowest level of fear being harbored within themselves. Thus, that is what they speak. From this, this gain some misguided sense of omnipotence.

Think about it, are you all alone? Are you in fear of being all alone? If you are, then you too may speak the aforementioned words. If you are not, then you would never articulate this type of insult.

But, this entire occurrence, and the man's reaction thereof, illustrates a bigger issue and it provides us with a reason to looking within ourselves. What are you afraid of? What do you internally fear? Look deeply into yourself. How do you see yourself? What flaws do you think you possess? How do you project those fears and those flaws to the world?

A person who is not whole onto themselves does not possess a clearly defined sense of discretion and an understanding of righteousness and, thus, they project negativity to the world. They want to take the focus off of themselves and place it somewhere, on someone else.

Look around your life, how many people do you know that spend their time thinking and talking about someone else—taking shots at someone else?

Criticism is easy? Anybody can say anything. Insults are easy. Making a criticism or an insult look like factual statement is a bit harder but it too is not difficult.

But, there is a problem that arises from this type of behavior. What these people are saying does not have to be true but because they are saying it their words enter it into the realms of physical reality. And, this is where the problems for humankind begin. People believe.

In this modern news cycle and political climate, the term, *"Fake news,"* has become highly bantered about. Yes, it has become of a bit of a catch-phase joke, but what it is describing is very valid and it is an important subject to contemplate. Most people believe what they hear. Thus, what anybody say has the potential to change the minds of anyone/everyone. True or false, factual or not, is almost unimportant. People believe… From what they believe a course of events is set into motion in their life and the lives of all those they interact with. But, what is never studied or never contemplated is who is saying what and why they saying it.

Why do you say what you say? Why do you say what you say about other people? Why do you believe what other people say? Do you ever take the time to think for yourself? Do you ever take the time to contemplate why the person who is saying something about something or to somebody is saying it at all? Do you ever dig deep into your own psyche and contemplate why you feel what you feel and why you say what you say?

Now, back to the original situation that motivated this blog... People, like that guy, say what they say, do their damage they do, and then they run away. Would the guy who accosted the elderly lady in that manner have said something like that to me? I doubt it. Would he have said it to the big burly guy who works in the meat department who is six-five and many two-seven-five, who stared the guy down as he walked away ranting? Doubtful... He said it because he could. ...Because he knew he could get over on that elderly lady. And, that is how the weak people operate.

Now, this brings us back to the point of, *"Fake news."* People say things, especially on places like the internet, because they will not need to face the consequences of their words. They say things, because they are hiding. They say them to the elderly because the do not have to fear being beaten down. They say them because they are not whole enough to be focused on forgiveness and the betterment of the world instead of focusing on someone or something else.

Moreover, whenever you hear anyone saying anything, you must remain focused on the question, *"Who is saying what and why?"* What motivates a person to say harsh words to an elderly lady. What motives a person to say harsh words to or about anybody? That is just wrong!

Though it is not right, it is wrong to say harsh words to anybody about any thing. Who are you to judge? Who is anybody to be cruel to any other person?

Most of us are nice. We would never accost an elderly lady in the manner that I speak about. But, there are some bad, unthinking, insecure people among us. Those who seek a method to unleash their own inner rage outwards. They are not good people. You should not listen to them. But, they are out there and you may have to encounter them from time to time. If and when you do, the best thing you can do is to not let their inner; self-loathing rage control you. You are more, so be more. Never fall prey to the words they speak.

A gentleman smiles and walks away.

Right Thought
09/Apr/2017 07:16 AM

One of the key components to living a spiritual life, as taught in Buddhism and other spiritual traditions, is the concept of, *"Right Thought."* But, what is Right Thought?

Right Thought is the practice of the individual taking control over their thinking mind, not being controlled by negative, detrimental, or desire-filled thoughts and, thus, thinking only focused, positive thoughts that lead to the betterment of the individual and the entire world.

Most people have no control over what they think. What they think is based solely upon what they are feeling, (about themselves and other people), what they want, how they want to be perceived by the world, and how they want other people to think—believing as they believe. Certainly, that is the short list of what causes a person to think in a certain manner but the fact is, few people ever take the time to even think about controlling what they are thinking.

The reason that it is important to embrace Right Thought is that what you think sets up and unleashes the pattern of experiences you will encounter throughout your entire life.

What you think about causes you to do what you to do. Therefore, if what you are thinking embraces the mindset of negativity, judgment, selfishness, self-righteousness, or immorality your thoughts will lead you to say and do bad things that will not only affect your own life in a negative manner but the lives of others, as well. Thus, not only is your entire life given birth to by what you think but what you think has the potential to spread out from your mind and effect the entire world.

What do you spend your time thinking about? How does what you think about affect your life? How has what you have thought about affected the lives of other people?

First, think about this... How has what you have done, based upon what you have thought, been the causation factor for what has happen in your life?

Now, ponder this... How has what you have done, based upon what you have thought, been the causation factor for what has happened to the life of the people you know and the lives of those people you have never met but have thought about?

Again, in life, what you think about causes you to do what you do. If what you do, based upon what you think, affects the life of any other person, in either a positive or a negative manner, you are one-hundred percent responsible for that occurrence. Thus, your thoughts equal your karma. It was you who thought the thought. It was you who took action because of what you thought. Thus, it will ultimately be you who must pay the karmic price for emulating and actualizing the thoughts you thought in your mind.

Now that you understand how the thoughts you think are elemental to the evolution of your life and the lives of those people you think about, it is time to decide to not only understand your thoughts and your thought patterns but to take control over what you think, as well.

To begin the process of Right Thought you must first decide to become very aware of what you are thinking. This is not as easy as it sounds. Again, most people never take the time to even contemplate what they are thinking or why— nor do they ever study the evolution of how their thoughts have lead to the actions they have taken in their life, leading to their overall life experience.

Do you think about what you think? Do you think about why you think it? If you want to embrace Right Thought, this is the first step you must take. Study your own mind.

Right now, take a moment, what are you thinking? Now, trace that thought back. Why are you thinking it? Is what you are thinking something that you believe? Is what you are thinking something someone told you to believe? Is what you are thinking something you want to believe? Is what you are thinking something that you once believed but believe no longer?

At each moment of your life this practice of consciously taking note of what you are thinking will lead you to a clear understanding of why you are thinking what you are thinking. Moreover, as you come to understand your own mind this practice will allow you to not only understand how the actions, based upon your thoughts, have lead to your previous life experience but how, through your focused thoughts, you can guide your life to the place where you want it to be.

Everything you think is based upon what you choose to think. Yes, there are a million things that have caused you to think the way you think but it is you who allows yourself to think those thoughts. Thus, at the heart of the practice of Right Thought is you deciding to take control over what you think and focus your thoughts to the degree where they only lead to the betterment of all.

Each of us in our lives experience both good and bad situations. These occurrences cause us to feel a certain way which thereby causes us to think in a particular manner. Experience equals thought. But, it is the mindful individual who does not allow the various life experiences, that we each encounter, to control the pattern of their thought. You live it. You feel it. It causes you to experience an emotion which leads you to thinking. But, it is the person who practices the techniques of Right Thought that never lets the emotions motivated by experience to come to dominate their mind and control what they are thinking. The person who practices Right Thought learns to consciously take control over all of their thoughts. Thus, they become whole and one-pointed thereby gaining a clearer understanding of Self and the cosmos.

You can be more. How can you become more? The first step is to take control of your thought. Think before you think.

If you wish to walk the pathway towards enlightenment, Right Thought is the first step.

My Time is Not Your Time
08/Apr/2017 07:59 AM

Have you ever had somebody contact you and tell you that they wanted you to do something for them? They didn't ask what you were doing or if you had the time to help them out—in fact they didn't even think about you at all, they just wanted something and they expected you to drop everything and do it?

Have you ever gone out of your way to help someone out—take the time to make their life a little easier or a bit better and they did not even take notice of the fact that you went out of your way to help them out? They didn't think of you or thank you but then they asked something more of you.

Have you ever decided to do something—thinking only about yourself: your life and your desires but what you did set a whole sting of chaotic events into motion in another person's life forcing them to lose their peace and spend a lot of their time thinking about and attempting to repair what you had done?

If we look at life we can easily see that we, as human beings, are an interactive breed. We want family, friends, and associates. Most of us want those to be friendly, cordial, and productive relationships. As such, we are happy to do things for other people when we can. Some people are not like that, however. They don't want to do anything for anyone. They only think about themselves. In fact, some people are simply blind and do not even care about how others are going out of their way to do things for them. They just take and then they expect more.

All of life is lived from what we know. What we know if based upon what we have experienced in life. Where we find ourselves in life is predicated upon a few factors, culture, age, socioeconomic status, but mostly upon how we choose to view and react to the world.

Caring and giving is a choice. As is expecting and taking.

A defined period of time is all that we have in this life. When it's gone; that's it, life is over! So, what we do with our time is of paramount importance.

Think about yourself... How do you spend your Life Time? How much of your time do you consciously give to others and how much of other people's time do you expect them to give to you?

Next time you ask someone to do something for you, think what that may be costing their life. Next time someone does something for you, without your asking, witness it, acknowledge it, realize that they could be doing something else, and mostly thank them.

This is life, our time is all we have.

You Can Say Anything That You Want but That Doesn't Make It True
07/Apr/2017 03:15 PM

I believe than in each of our lives we have encountered somebody saying something about someone or something and, in many cases, they present their words as fact. But are they?

I believe that many of us want to believe what we hear when other people are speaking. We are trusting and we want to believe in the goodness of people. Why would they lie?

But, people do lie. People do present what they believe as the truth when it is far from it. People do want to hurt the lives of other people via their words. Yes, what they speak may be their opinion. But, an opinion is never the truth. It is simply what one person believes to be the truth.

This is an important distinction to make when you listen to the words of others. Sure, they may actually believe everything they are saying to be based in the truth but it is most likely simply their truth and not the universal truth.

But, what actually is the truth? If life is based upon each person's interpretation of reality, defined by what they believe, then where does the absolute definition of truth arise?

This is a complicated question as most people are set up with a predetermined set of beliefs when they are young and few ever veer very away from this belief system. Yes, they grow up, have their own experiences, and develop their own personality. But, if you look to any person's individual evolution, what they actually do in their life is highly defined by how they were trained to react to the world when they were children and from this comes their understanding of what is or is not the truth.

The fact is, most people cannot consciously differentiate between their opinion and the truth. They simply believe what they believe, based upon the facts that they choose to calculate, and from this, they then define their reality which they spread out to the world.

Think about it... What do you believe and why do you believe it? When you hear someone say something, do you simply take them at their word or do you dig deeper, finding your own truth in the actual facts that are obtainable?

Most people are life lazy. The don't want to think. They don't want to analyze. They simply want to be told. If they like what they hear, if what they hear provides them with a sense of enjoyment, fulfillment, purpose, or it strokes their emotions in a way they want them to be stroked then seeking the truth becomes completely unimportant. What they hear is all they need to know. End of story... They believe.

This is a complicated place to live your life from, however. For if you simply believe, then there is no doubt that you will be lied to. And, in fact, you may re-spread that lie because you may re-speak it to other people. Thus, that lie spreads across all of existence.

Have you ever believed something but then you changed your mind? I think that most of us have experienced this in our lives. We heard, we believed, and then we spoke what we believed. But, then we believed it no more. Now what?

Think about it, there are probably still people out there believing what you said and, thus, your belief became their belief and their belief became the belief of others that they spread it to. This, when you no longer believe it. How do you think that will ultimately affect your life evolution and your overall karma?

Have you ever watched someone who once told everyone how something was good or true and then they changed their mind and they tried to justify why they spoke the words that they had previously spoken? Have you ever watched them squirm and look for a logical, justifiable reason why they said what they said? This, after what they said may have negatively affected the lives of many people. Yet, they still try to justify their words and remove themselves from any ultimate responsibility. Maybe they even lie to hide from their responsibility. But, what they said is what they said. How what they said affected the lives of others is how it affected the lives of others. Now what?

Then, there are other people that simply don't care. They say what they say based upon whatever motivating emotion they may be experiencing. It may be the truth. It may be a lie. It may hurt the life of other people but they are so self-involved that they hold a devil-may-care attitude and all others be damned. "I think it. I said it, So what!" That's not good. You really need to watch out for people like that. It is easy to see them and detect this personality trait. They are the ones who are constantly casting judgment while attempting to make their opinion seem factional as their words damage the lives of others.

Some people consciously lie. They lie to make themselves appear to something more than they actually are. Others people don't mean to lie but by believing what they believe they spread a lie. Some people live solely in the world of opinion—believing that their opinion is the truth when all they are speaking is an opinion. Yet, many people are not aware enough to realize this. Thus, they cannot and do not present anyone with this fact. They simply spread their opinion as truth when it is far from it.

With all this being said, how do you encounter life? Do you believe all you hear? Do you tell other people what your opinion is but speak it as the truth? Do you tell people what they should do based upon your own life experiences? If you do this, how are your responsible for what they encounter in life? How? It makes you totally karmically responsible.

Ultimately, your life is not the life of anyone else. What you know to be true can never be the truth of another person. Yes, you may find a common ground with a certain person or a certain group but no-one is you. Thus, the only true truth is what you can know from your own personal life realizations. No truth can be given to you. And, you cannot tell anyone else what is the truth. Yes, you can believe what another person says if you want to. But, as you have no doubt experienced in your own life, what you believe may change. Thus, belief is never the truth. At best, what someone tells you is simply their understanding of life defined by what they have experienced. But, what they have experienced is never what you will experience.

Ultimately, there is no one truth. Your truth is not my truth. My truth is not your truth. Be silent and do no damage to the life of others by telling anyone what you think that you believe. As any damage you create by speaking what you believe will only come back to haunt you. Let each person be whole onto themselves.

Be more. Be yourself. Know your own truth. Be silent.

I Believe in You
07/Apr/2017 08:57 AM

Have you ever had somebody say, *"I believe in you?"* But, what does that actually mean? What does believing in somebody entail? And, how does, "Believing in," affect the life of the believer and the life of the believed in?

People believe in god. God—that abstract ideology that promises an eternity in heaven if you are good and follow the rules in life. People believe in the devil. Satan—the abstract ideology who will send your soul through never ending damnation if you are bad in life. People believe in superstition—that abstract ideology that, "If some particular something happens," it signals what will come next. Some people construct their whole life around believing in superstition. Some people believe in the words of a teachers. They believe them until they no longer believe in that person once they have discovered that individual's flaws. But, does what a person believes in make their belief true? Or, is it simply something to get them through their day, either in a more positive and productive manner or through embracing negative beliefs which engulfs them via adrenalized rage giving birth to a feeling of false empowerment?

Belief is belief. But, what does it mean? We all believe in what we believe in. Is what you believe right and true or is simply what you believe? What about others who don't believe what you believe; are they wrong? And, if so, what does that mean to their life? What does that mean to your life?

"I believe in you." When you believe in someone what does that make you do? How do you act and react to that person? What do you give them because you believe in them? Does you believing in them change anything in their life? And, if you didn't believe in them or you decide you no

longer believe in them, how will that affect their life and how will that affect your life?

Belief is a strange concept as it is only, *"Believed,"* in the mind of the individual. But, how does that belief (how does your belief) translate out to the world? How does it affect the world on the whole? How does it affect the people you believe in? And, does your believing in someone or something change anything at all?

What does your mind believe? How does what believe control your life? What does it make you do? And, how will what you do, based upon what you believe, affect the rest of your life and the life or lives of those you supposedly believe in?

* * *

06/Apr/2017 07:16 AM

How much of what you have done in the past do you hide from, lie about, or pretend didn't happen?

*   *   *
06/Apr/2017 07:13 AM

You remember what you remember. When your life is over who will remember it?

In This Moment is Everything
05/Apr/2017 08:35 AM

Do you ever find yourself sitting back, taking a look around, studying your environment and realizing that all is well with the world—you are happy, life is okay, and everything is as it should be?

Do you ever find yourself sitting back and being really angry at what someone has done to you, what someone has said about you, or that your life is just not going the way you want it to go?

What is the difference between these two states of mind? The first, you are getting what you want, you are encountering no life resistance, and no controversy or catastrophe is coming your direction. You are whole, complete, and fulfilled in your moment. The second, you are encountering the unwanted realities of life. You are confronted with the fact that most people are not nice, nor are they caring. In fact, most people do not care about anybody but themselves. From this, the world of damage, anger, frustration, and chaos is given birth to.

But, there is more to it than this. There is more to experiencing life experience than simply being controlled by it.

There you are living your moment... You are feeling what you are feeling, based upon what you are experiencing. What can you learn from this? What you can learn is that life is created by where you place your self and how you choose to react to each life stimuli.

For most of us, we are born into a world, a historic time period, a financial determinant, and a culture that we had no choice in choosing. We are given life and where we are given life is what we must contend with. Some, have all things provided for them: a good family, health, beauty, money, and a promising future. Most of us are not like that, however. Most of us are placed in a life where we must learn to accept our life-shortcomings and our life-limitations. And, then deal with the repercussions that are born from them.

Okay, but now what? How are you going to react to what you have been given and what you are experience in a world dominated by what you were given?

You are given what you are given. But, it is what you do with what you are given than defines your life. Your life is dominated and created by the choices you make, defined by what you were given.

If you find yourself in a world of happiness, how are you responsible for that? If you discover yourself is a world of anger or saddens, how are you responsible for that? How did you come to where you are? You arrived there, defined by the choices you made within the realm of what you were given?

You made choices. You ended up where you are not only calculated by your life-determinates but more probably by the choices you have made.

Have you seen a very poor person be happy? Have you seen a very wealthy individual be sad? Thus, it is easy to see, what you have out there is not necessarily the determining factor for what you feel in here.

Your life is constructed by how you encounter your life and what you choose to do with the life-determinates you are given.

Where do you find yourself right now in your life? Are you happy, fulfilled, content? Or, are you angry, frustration, and miserable? These are your emotions. Nobody else is feeling them but you. Thus, nobody cares about what you are feeling. But now, look at it this way; instead of simply feeling your emotions and being dominated by them you must become self aware enough to understand that it was and is you who choose to lead your life to a place where you will encounter the emotions you are feeling based upon the people, the life, and the life style that you have surrounded yourself with.

Therefore, to ever gain any control over your life, you must first realize and accept it was you who got you to where you are in the first place. Blame no one else. You made choices. They were your choices. Now, take responsibility for them. Moreover, learn to take control over them as it is from your emotions, motivated by the choices you made, that the next level of your entire life is created.

When you are happy, you think, say, and do good things. When you are angry, frustrated, sad; these emotions also dominate how you react to the world. The difference is, the negative emotions are what causes you to do bad things that hurt other people. If you hurt other people, based upon what you are feeling, how do you think that will impact the rest of your life? Do you think there are no repercussions for the actions your take based upon whatever desire or self-involved emotion you are experiencing? Believe me, there are.

What you do now equals your tomorrow. What you feel now sets the standard for what you will feel tomorrow.

Your life is created by what you choose to do with what you are given. Your emotions: happy or sad, are created by how you choose to experience the life you have created for yourself defined by the choices you have made.

When you find yourself sitting back and realizing you are encountering joy, simply by experiencing your world as it is, embrace it. When you find yourself sitting back and realizing that you discontent, sad or angry, don't lash out; instead, chose to change you. …As you are the sourcepoint for all that you feel.

Never let your negative emotions control you or your actions. Consciously move yourself, through the choices you make, to a place when you transcend the negative elements of your emotions and move yourself to a world where your happiness can be embraced.

Joy and happiness are everywhere. There is no drug you need to take to feel them. But, there is a drug you need to take when you are experiencing the opposite of joy and happiness. That drug is you looking at the choices you have made and then redefining your life to make better choices so that less than ideal emotions never need be encountered due to the choices you have made.

In this moment is everything. You can be whole, happy, fulfilled, and blissful. All you have to do is to chose to experience it.

A New Reason to Run
05/Apr/2017 08:28 AM

I was cruising down 6th St., over by Alvarado, last week. I was coming from Tommy's, having had the/my traditional Double Chili/Cheese, a bag of barbecue chips, and a bottled water. I was heading over to this thrift store I like to check out when I'm in the neighborhood. I was driving on the inside lane, the music was on, and all was well with the world. All of a sudden this guy in his mini van abruptly changes lanes into my lane. I hit the horn, slam on my breaks, and skid for a long way. As he was coming right at me without stopping, I was trying to avoid him hitting me so I was veering to the right. Finally, I came to a stop. But, he kept driving. I got out of my car to make sure that I had not hit the parked car next to where I finally stopped. Looking, I was literally just about a half an inch away from it. But, as there was no damage, I get back in my car in order to chase down the guy. I caught up to him at a stop light about a mile away. I get out of the car, take a photo of his license plate, and was screaming at him like a maniac. His window was down, he heard me, he knew what he had done, but he darted off.

Recently, with our new president here in the States, there has been a lot of talk about the deportation of undocumented immigrants. Now, I'm not going to get into that debate here because everyone has their opinion. I will say, if you look at it from a more personal perspective; ask yourself, *"How would you feel if you were happily living in your house and you came home one day and somebody had moved in. You didn't want them there, you didn't ask them to move in, yet they arrived, they were living at your home, and they will not leave. Next, they invited their family to move into your house and now their family will not leave. How would you feel?"*

Okay, but back to the storyline… For any of us who drive a car, especially in a large urban center like Los Angeles, you are probably going to have gotten into a fender bender or two. Not good. But, people make mistakes. Now, I have had people take off when they have hit my car more than once and that is not cool. But now, today, in this political landscape, people are taking off for a whole new reason; i.e. they are illegal immigrants and they are afraid of being deported for the smallest of reasons—as that is what is currently happening. Thus, people have found a whole new reason to run.

Now certainly, I was driving through a crappy part of town, inhabited predominately by people of Latin descent, of which a large percentage are undocumented. But, that is no excuse to not take responsibility for what you have done in and with your life. And, here lies the ultimate definition of the life you live… What you do defines who you are. What you say to people, what you say about people, how you react to the world, and what you give back to the world sets the definition for your life. We can all find reasons to not want to take responsibility for the mistakes we have made. That is why we must live life as consciously as possible, as righteously as possible—consciously only saying and doing good things so we will not have that many mistakes to own up to. But, when you do make a mistake, it is what you do to fix that mistake that defines you as a human being.

You must ask yourself, *"Who are you? What are You? Are you the person who unleashes negativity and damage, no matter what the logic, reasoning, or excuse? Or, are you a person who consciously encounters life and when you do say or do something that damages the life of another person you care enough to care and you take responsible and repair any damage you have created?"*

If you are living your life from a perspective where you must run from your mistakes, you are living in the wrong world. We all make mistakes, but if you are a good and conscious person you fix anything that you have broken.

I'm the Only Person Who Remembers My Father
04/Apr/2017 12:43 PM

I was driving past the Long Beach Municipal Cemetery today. I had actually shot a scene for one of my Zen Films there, (at night), about a year and a half ago. As I drove by I took notice of and remembered how all of the large headstone were symbolizing the lives of people that had died many years ago. It is an old cemetery. The thought came to my mind that there is probably nobody left alive who even remembers any of those people. Then, I realized, I am the only person alive who actually remembers my father.

My father passed away in 1968. He actually died at the Los Angeles Forum, inside the Forum Club, from a massive heart attack. At the time, he was the general manager of The Forum. Prior to that, he had owned a very successful restaurant near the U.S.C. campus that he had sold, planning to retire young, as he had already had one heart attack at the age of forty-four. But, he didn't like retirement so he got another job. Thus, he lived and he died on the job.

Though at both of those established he had made a lot of friends, I realized today, that most people don't live to be a hundred, as such, all of his friends and contemporaries would be dead. As I was an only child, having a small extended family, that's it—it's me, the only one left alive who actually remembers him.

This is an important thing to keep in mind as you pass through your life. You will live, you will do what you do, but then you will die. Who will remember you after you pass away? Why will they remember you? How long will you be remembered?

* * *
11/Mar/2017 05:14 PM

The truth is never a lie.

*   *   *

11/Mar/2017 05:14 PM

You don't learn the rules of the game until you play the game.

* * *

11/Mar/2017 05:13 PM

Who are you and what have you done with your life?

*   *   *
10/Mar/2017 08:23 AM

When you do something bad and there is no one there to witness it do you think that makes it okay?

All actions have consequences.

*   *   *

10/Mar/2017 07:37 AM

Does the squirrel running through the field care what you're going through?

* * *
07/Mar/2017 06:51 AM

For every bad situation that occurs in your life if you look back through time you will realizing that it began by one choice being made and most often that choice was made by you.

* * *
07/Mar/2017 06:50 AM

If you were going to die tomorrow how many apologies would you have to make? That number is a good definition of how you are living your life.

*   *   *
04/Mar/2017 07:38 AM

When you are the only one who knows the truth if you tell someone else will they even believe you?

*   *   *

23/Feb/2017 09:38 AM

If you don't know what you want out of life you can't get it.

If you do know what you want out of life you probably won't get it.

Now what?

* * *
09/Feb/2017 01:32 PM

Life Philosophy in a Nutshell:

Say only good things. Do only good things. Help everyone you can.

Never judge anyone—their accomplishments or their creations.

Don't tell lies.

Never intentionally hurt anyone for any reason.

If you do hurt someone apologize and do all that you can to repair any damage that you've inflicted.

* * *
08/Feb/2017 12:06 PM

If you were going to die tomorrow what would you do today?

If you live your life embracing this mindset your everyday existence becomes far more accomplished.

*   *   *
07/Feb/2017 12:05 PM

Do all of the good deeds you do today erase that one bad thing you did way back when?

* * *
06/Feb/2017 01:05 PM

You should really stop dreaming about the dreams that will never come true.

THE
ZEN

www.ingramcontent.com/pod-product-compliance
Lightning Source LLC
Chambersburg PA
CBHW070638170426
43200CB00010B/2058